1973

Twayne's United States Authors Series

Sylvia E. Bowman, *Editor*

INDIANA UNIVERSITY

Caroline M. Kirkland

CAROLINE M. KIRKLAND

By WILLIAM S. OSBORNE

Southern Connecticut State College

 207

Twayne Publishers, Inc.   ::   New York

FOR RUTH

Preface

WITH the publication of *A New Home—Who'll Follow?* (1839), Mrs. Caroline M. Kirkland found that she was suddenly—in Edgar Allan Poe's words—"at the head of American female authors." Although Michigan neighbors objected to the frank portrait of life in a raw pioneer village of the emerging Middle West, the critics and the reading public in the East took delight in her intimate narrative. *A New Home* was the first book to suggest the exuberant—sometimes exasperating—spirit of the American wilderness. Poe, writing in "The Literati of New York City," summarized the general opinion: "to Mrs. Kirkland alone we [are] indebted for our acquaintance with the *home* and home-life of our backwoodsman."

The immediate acclaim given *A New Home* prompted Mrs. Kirkland to write *Forest Life* (1842), a more deliberate study of Western life and manners, and to prepare *Western Clearings* (1846), a collection of essays and tales about Michigan which she had already published in women's magazines. When she and her husband returned to New York after their sojourn in the West, she settled easily into a writing routine which gave her only a modest income but which secured for her steady access as contributor to the magazines because editors were eager to have her work. She was versatile enough to supply what commanded their attention and what satisfied the women readers: more Western sketches, sentimental tales, and instructive essays.

Although she never surpassed the literary achievements of *A New Home* and *Forest Life,* in the 1840's and 1850's she was one of the most popular and highly respected women writers in America. Her services were much in demand. She was editor of one of the better magazines, *The Union Magazine of Literature and Art;* and she published three gift books (collections of her essays which had appeared in the magazines), several anthologies of poetry (especially appealing to women), and a biography of Washington for young people.

The danger in so much labor for the magazines and in supplying the kind of material popular with the women readers in mid-nineteenth-century America is that writing standards change; and the writer—no matter how distinguished in one's own day—is too soon forgotten. After the passage of years, Mrs. Kirkland was judged a writer of pleasant, instructive, tasteful essays for the time but not an impressive one in the long view. Her reputation hardly outlived her.

What is indeed unfortunate is that her sketches of the Middle West in *A New Home* and *Forest Life,* and perhaps *Western Clearings,* have been neglected as pioneer work in the development of American realism. Even Mrs. Kirkland seemed to overlook what her Western studies had accomplished for American writing: she ignored the romantic tendency in the prose of her day, adopted a simpler style, and wrote frankly of life as it was—thereby anticipating the vitality in fiction that was to figure so strongly in American writing in the post-Civil War years.

This study, then, is a record of Mrs. Kirkland's accomplishments: an analysis of her regional sketches, which are truly significant, and a review of the better material she wrote for women's magazines.

Since an edition of *A New Home* is readily available, I have confined my comments in the chapter on Mrs. Kirkland's first book to her ideas and personal impressions of the West, leaving the reader the delight of discovering much of her narrative for himself. I have been deliberately detailed in the chapter on *Forest Life* because it is the first book to employ the regionalist's view of material and because it is not immediately available to the reader, except in libraries. *Western Clearings* is not the book its predecessors were; although I have devoted less attention to it, I have tried to suggest its content.

I have exercised selectivity in discussing Mrs. Kirkland's magazine material and have quoted liberally from the articles because they are not readily accessible to the reader. Much of the material may be ephemeral (in that its appeal was primarily to women of nineteenth-century America); nevertheless, it is representative of the sketches, tales, and essays which appeared in the magazines during the decades when magazines in America were largely the province of women. I have prepared a bibliography of Mrs. Kirkland's essays and fiction published in the magazines; other material not listed in the bibliography can be found in *Western Clearings* and in the three annuals: *The Evening Book, A Book for the Home Circle,* and *Autumn Hours.*

There is not a great deal of primary source material; many family records were apparently lost in the Chicago fire (her children were living in Chicago at the time). Much of the information about Mrs. Kirkland until the time of her departure from Michigan comes from two valuable sources: Langley C. Keyes's *Caroline M. Kirkland: A Pioneer in American Realism,* a doctoral dissertation at Harvard University (1935); and Mrs. Louise N. Knudsen's *Caroline Kirkland, Pioneer,* a master's thesis at Michigan State College of Agriculture and Applied Science (1934). The emphasis in both these studies is primarily on the formative years and on the years spent in the West. Other information comes from some hundred-odd letters written by Mrs. Kirkland which are deposited in libraries throughout the country. These sources are liberally quoted because I feel they help to identify Mrs. Kirkland as a person and to tell something about the times in which she as a woman writer had to live.

I wish to thank Professor Sylvia E. Bowman who first gave me the encouragement and then the pleasant assignment of writing this study. I am indeed grateful for permission to quote in the book the letters of Mrs. Kirkland, which have found their way into so many libraries throughout the country: Boston Public Library; Newberry Library, Chicago; University of Chicago Library; Cornell University Library; Baker Memorial Library, Dartmouth College; Widener Memorial Library, Harvard University; Charles Roberts Autograph Collection, Haverford College; Henry E. Huntington Library; Johns Hopkins University Library; Massachusetts Historical Society; William L. Clements Library, University of Michigan; Michigan Historical Collections, University of Michigan; Bryant-Godwin Collection, Duyckinck Collection and Miscellaneous Manuscript Collection in the New York Public Library; Historical Society of Pennsylvania; Clifton Waller Barrett Library, University of Virginia; Sterling Memorial Library, Yale University.

I wish to thank also Mr. I. Frederick Doduck for permission to use material already published in the College and University

Press edition of *A New Home,* and Mrs. Susan B. Dunn in the Library of Southern Connecticut State College for assistance in procuring research materials for me.

WILLIAM S. OSBORNE

Wallingford, Connecticut

Contents

Chronology

1801 Caroline Matilda Stansbury born on January 11; eldest daughter of Samuel Stansbury and Eliza Alexander Stansbury.

1809 Attended Quaker school established by her aunt, Mrs. Lydia Philadelphia Mott.

1814– Student and then assistant in another school operated by
1819 Mrs. Mott, a boarding school near Utica, New York; met William Kirkland.

1822 Father died; widowed mother and children moved to Clinton, New York, where Caroline was nearer her fiancé William Kirkland, an instructor at Hamilton College.

1825– Kirkland abroad on two-year study program.
1827

1828 Married William Kirkland on January 10; the couple opened a seminary in Geneva, New York.

1830 First son (second child) Joseph Kirkland, born on January 7.

1835 Left upstate New York for Michigan Territory where Kirkland had been appointed principal of Detroit Female Seminary; wife also taught in the school.

1836 Kirkland began buying land in Livingston County, sixty miles west of Detroit; accumulated 1,300 acres over period of year and a half; planned village of Pinckney.

1837 Mother died; Kirklands moved to Pinckney.

1839 *A New Home—Who'll Follow?* published.

1840 Articles accepted for publication in women's magazines.

1842 *Forest Life* published.

1843 Kirklands returned to New York City, where both wrote for magazines and opened a school.

1846 *Western Clearings* published; William Kirkland died on October 18.

1847   *Spenser and the Faery Queen* published; editor of *Union Magazine* for next year and a half.

1848   First trip to Europe.

1849   *Holidays Abroad; or, Europe from the West* published; now associate editor, with John S. Hart, of *Union Magazine;* contributed to *Union* and also to other periodicals.

1850   Second trip to Europe.

1852   *The Evening Book, Garden Walks with the Poets,* and *The Book of Home Beauty* published; essay on William Cullen Bryant for *Homes of American Authors;* began teaching again, intermittently, for rest of decade.

1853   *A Book for the Home Circle* and *The Helping Hand* published; associated with *Putnam's Monthly.*

1854   *Autumn Hours* published; essay on George Washington for *Homes of American Statesmen.*

1857   *Personal Memoirs of George Washington* published.

1861   War work, particularly for United States Sanitary Commission.

1864   *The School-Girl's Garland* published; active in Metropolitan Fair for benefit of Sanitary Commission; died on April 6.

CHAPTER *1*

"All Pleasant and Good Thoughts"

"I THANK you, my love, for your . . . letter—it was all I could wish, and soothed my feelings most delightfully," wrote Caroline Matilda Stansbury on Christmas Day, 1826, to her fiancé William Kirkland, who was still abroad on a two-year program of study. "I have been suffering much from an apprehension that your affection for me was declining—that you had made reputation your idol—and that your engagement was a burthen to you," she teased ever so carefully; then she more seriously added, "but the expressions you give me . . . have comforted me, and I feel once more reassured of your enduring affection." [1] Caroline's "suffering"—a deep concern over her fiancé's state of mind, one greatly agitated by his personal problems when he had left her over a year before—was relieved by the letter "so full of love and sympathy."

"To tell the truth," she continued, "before the arrival of the [letter] my affection for you was in some degree deadened—the coldness which is almost unavoidable in a correspondence by letter, had in the lapse of 16 months, effaced many of those little tender recollections which are the very life of love. I still preferred you to all the world and felt willing to sacrifice anything for your sake," she avowed; "but there was a chill came over me whenever I thought of the change which two years absence *might* make in your person—in your habits and manners—but above all in your feelings toward me. But your . . . letter . . . [has] renewed in my heart a conviction that nothing but death can or ought to separate us. . . . let nothing," she confidently admonished, "prevent your return at the appointed time." [2]

The letter revealed facets of personality which Caroline M. Kirkland exhibited throughout life—by turns, a frankness which could be disarming; a tenderness which was always sincere; a warmth of feeling which she showed easily to those whom she

admired or loved; a strength of will which on occasion caused
embarrassment to her and consternation to her family and her
friends. She was a young woman of twenty-five when she wrote
this letter to William Kirkland. A vigorous young woman, she
sought lively companionship and confronted experience directly,
often with ready wit; but she was also a somewhat eager young
woman thinly hiding anxieties which could be real enough.

I *"Our Dear Little Poppet"* [3]

Caroline Matilda Stansbury was born January 11, 1801, in New
York City, the eldest of the eleven children of Samuel and Eliza
(Alexander) Stansbury. From her mother, she obviously learned
the feminine graces: tenderness and sympathy, gentility, and love
of virtue. Mrs. Stansbury was fond of reading romances and poetry and even wrote a few sentimental pieces which her daughter
edited and published years later in the books she prepared for
women readers.[4] The sentimental strain so strong in Caroline M.
Kirkland's magazine fiction—the very strain that today condemns
this writing to dusty library stacks—was nourished by Mrs. Stansbury's predilection to this singularly feminine manner of expression.

The livelier strain in Caroline M. Kirkland's writing—the fresh,
exuberant strain so markedly present in *A New Home,* in *Forest
Life,* and in the best of the Western sketches—was stimulated by
her father and particularly by her grandfather Joseph Stansbury,
a staunch Loyalist who during the American Revolution had published satiric verses under the pseudonym Roderick Random in
Rivington's *Royal Gazette.* She had doubtless read her grandfather's political songs and satiric verses—"characterized by playful
humor rather than by hatred," opined Moses Coit Tyler, who appreciated Joseph Stansbury's talent if not his Tory persuasion[5]—
and learned in part from him how to use her own satiric gift.
Something in the grandfather's frankness and zest for life de-
scended to her as well.

Samuel Stansbury, her father, needed his share of shrewd wit to
buttress the misfortunes in business he engaged in to support a
growing family. A jack-of-all-trades and seemingly master of
none, Samuel Stansbury was by turns a clerk in several dry-goods
stores, in a hardware store, and in a bank. At the time of his marriage, he was working for an insurance company in New York. In

1804, when Caroline was a child of three, he moved the family to Greenwich, Connecticut, and opened a stationery and book store; in five years, deeply in debt, he lost the store and moved the family back to New York,[6] where he resumed his former job with the insurance company.

Caroline was perhaps the father's favorite child, because her "versatile nature and witty turns of speech were so much like his own." [7] And the elder Stansbury's apparent love of books led him to instill a respect for knowledge in his daughter; indeed, he and his sister Lydia P. Mott superintended the girl's formal education. Mrs. Mott had married a Philadelphia Quaker, Robert Mott; had become a Quaker herself; and was headmistress of a number of seminaries, each distinguished for its sound curriculum. Caroline was a student in several of her aunt's schools; and, by the time she was ten, her father was writing that "she is now head of most of the classes in the School and in French so far superior as to study alone." [8] It was an aunt's affection and a teacher's pride that prompted Mrs. Mott to write so warmly to her brother and sister-in-law about her pupil:

> I hope the ease & confidence my dear Brother & Sister felt in placing their treasure with us does not lessen, & also hope it will not be disappointed, it is no trifling one for we are of the opinion that it may be called a double one, which compared to the general run of our scholars, as we think she has about twice as much in her as any we have got & needs about double the care; she is indeed as S. S. says "no common child." I am glad to find I have an ascendency over her.[9]

Mrs. Mott was an admirable teacher, and Caroline was a bright scholar—acquiring a very good command of Latin and French (as her writing shows), learning Greek and German, discovering an interest in literature and a talent for expression, and also demonstrating considerable grace in the more elegant accomplishments expected of young ladies in her day: music, drawing, dance. Her father once remarked in measured understatement: "the Diamond pin is well & lively as usual, I think gradually acquiring that steadiness . . . [which] alone is wanting to make her a fine girl." [10]

Caroline's high regard for knowledge, her own native ability, and the encouragement she was given by her father and her aunt made possible an education not every young girl in New York during that period had the advantage of having. In her late teens she began teaching in her aunt's Quaker school, one located in New Hartford, near Utica, New York, where she met William Kirkland. Mrs. Mott's Quakerism was a strong force in Caroline M. Kirkland's life: she devoted as much time and energy to teaching in her adult career as she did to writing; she espoused a number of charitable and reform movements in New York; she habitually inserted a strong humanitarian feeling in the essays she later prepared for the women's magazines.

II *The "Acquiring [of] Steadiness"*

The social position of the Stansburys in New York during their daughter's formative years remained secure and genteel in spite of the father's lack of success in business and the growing demands of an increasing family. They were city people, liberal in their views on education and culture yet conservative in politics and distrustful of radical elements in America's youthful society. They carefully nurtured Caroline's love of literature and her sensitive mind by good books, sophisticated tastes, sympathetic guidance. The Stansbury home, whether in poverty or prosperity, was one where formal education was "vitally supplemented by daily talks round the dinner table." [11] Caroline sharpened her wit and acquired some wisdom at these dinner-table sessions; yet she was apparently more than just an alert young woman capable of the right *bon mot*, more than just the brilliant scholar, for she had a large circle of friends and acquaintances attracted to her by many of those qualities one finds in her best writing—a vivacious manner, a kindness of heart, and a lively sense of humor.

After Samuel Stansbury was striken with paralysis in 1820, he suffered declining health until he died in New Haven, Connecticut, in the spring of 1822—a few months after Caroline's twenty-first birthday. The widowed mother, left with a large family to superintend, delegated many domestic and financial arrangements to her eldest daughter—a responsibility which matured Caroline in practical affairs and developed a confident manner in her association with people. For a time she was teaching in her aunt's school in upstate New York; yet separation from her mother, younger sisters, and brothers no doubt prompted her to urge Mrs. Stansbury to leave the metropolitan area for rural New

York. Moreover, Caroline was persuasive on several other counts: the family was already reduced by the death of the father and by the absence of the eldest son Joseph (who had left America to live and die in England); her mother's health was not strong; the family income (from some unaccountable source) would more nearly cover the demands of educating younger brothers at the recently founded college in the village of Clinton—Hamilton College; and living expenses would not be nearly so high in the country. What proved to be the most formidable reason, however, was that she was now engaged to a young man who lived in Clinton, and she obviously wished to be near him. Mrs. Stansbury hesitantly acceded to her daughter's argument; the family moved to the upstate village later in the year 1822. Determination had won out as it had with tradesmen and reluctant pupils; and a headstrong young woman, very much in love, convinced Mrs. Stansbury that she could, with feminine propriety, make the move.[12]

William Kirkland, small in stature, was a scholarly young man who had been appointed a tutor in the Classics at Hamilton in 1820, a position he held when Caroline met him. He came from a distinguished family of New England educators. A granduncle had been a missionary-teacher among the Indians in upstate New York and had obtained a charter for a school in which Indian and white boys were to be educated; when the school had proved impractical, it was re-chartered as Hamilton College.[13] His uncle John Thornton Kirkland was president of Harvard University from 1810 to 1828. His father Joseph Kirkland, a Yale graduate, had practiced law in Connecticut before moving to upstate New York where he began a political career that won him, at one point, election to Congress. He was the first mayor of Utica, New York, a general in the state militia, and a trustee of Hamilton College.

William Kirkland had graduated second in his class from the college in 1818. As an undergraduate, he had shown interest in Unitarian doctrines; his parents had advised travel in Europe, where he was also to study modern languages. If Rufus W. Griswold is right when he said that young Kirkland was educated for the ministry but that "some conscientious scruples kept him from ordination," [14] conjecture allows one to suggest that the same points of traditional doctrine may have troubled him as they did his more eminent contemporary Ralph Waldo Emerson, who also discovered some years later that a European tour was the right

experience for a man deeply agitated by scruples of conscience
and by his conflict with Congregational polity. At any rate, Kirkland, on his return from Europe in 1820, had accepted a teaching
assignment at Hamilton.

A mild-mannered young man who wore thick glasses to coun-
teract very poor eyesight, Kirkland had an energetic, restless
nature. His family connections and his scholarly inclination seemingly assured a bright future at the college. But an accident occurred that changed the whole course of his life when, as a college
prank, some students living in the dormitory where Kirkland was
in charge fired a small cannon in the hall outside the room where
he slept. The explosion not only caused considerable damage to
the building but permanently impaired the young instructor's
hearing. The way in which the incident was handled, as it was reported in a contemporary account, precipitated an open quarrel
between the trustees and the president and his faculty.

> A portion of the trustees wished the President to resign, which he
> distinctly refused to do, on the ground that his reputation was too
> deeply concerned to permit such a course. Year after year of
> crimination and recrimination passed between a majority of the
> board and the President; and as a house divided against itself can-
> not stand, so, in the years 1829 and 1830 there was no graduating
> class. During a portion of these years, the college was reduced
> to nine students, and a part, perhaps all of these, were induced to
> remain to save the charter of the institution.[15]

Kirkland, as well as Caroline, doubtless suffered humiliation,
anger, and then despair in the months that followed the cannon
episode; for the wrangling between the faculty and the trustees
was painful personally and academically. Though he stayed on at
the college for a time after the accident, he must have felt that a
heavy blow had been dealt a promising career; for deafness severely restricted his opportunity as a successful college teacher. In
the midst of the dissension at Hamilton, he requested a two-year
leave of absence to study abroad; the leave was granted, and he
left Clinton in 1825 to study in Germany.

Before Kirkland's sojourn in Europe was over, the dissension at
Hamilton had reached such a point of "crimination and recrimina-
tion" that the young man felt compelled to submit his resignation:

I have written my father [he informed Caroline from London in the spring of 1827] fully on the subject and given his full power to tender my resignation, which he seems to think indispensable, and in which opinion I coincide with him under present appearances. But you will say and I too say to myself, where does that place us? In a worse state, it is true, than having a *good* situation, but not worse than having a place in the college as at present constituted. But I will not despond and though I do not see at the present time exactly what is to become, yet shall I not cease hoping, that something may be done—something that shall enable us to join hands as well as hearts and no longer to defer our hopes. I shall not wait . . . for an assurance of a handsome support—a reasonable prospect of a comfortable subsistence will satisfy me and I doubt not, will satisfy you, and what we lack of the elegances and splendors of life, will be made up by our devoted affection and the moderation of our wishes. All I ask is *to see my way,* and I am sure my exertions will not be wanting to combat the obstacles it presents. Let us hope . . . for the best, nor be dismayed by the circumstances of the college, which may, after all, prove in the end, a happy deliverance. With the men at present there I can never harmonize and it is better, even at some personal sacrifice, to be elsewhere. . . . [I] bid you with the utmost sincerity, be of good cheer.[16]

Caroline's private feelings for Kirkland's disappointment were never shown; to him at least her stoic and resourceful nature was the equal of her fiancé. His return now was only a few months off—"I shall write you from New York the first moment after I get there," he went on to say in the letter, "and also write home with directions to take you prisoner and guard you well in our mansion (for fear of your running away) till I have you secure in my own possession. See what a good girl you can be till I come, when we shall be happier than tongue can tell." [17]

Caroline could rest more quietly now that her fiancé's mind was firmly on her injunction "to let nothing prevent your return at the appointed time." If one looks between the lines in the extant letters during the two-year separation, he sees often her anxiety over his mental state that had been induced by his extreme nearsightedness, his deafness, and his loss of profession. Lighthearted and affectionate she was determined to be; but uneasiness can be read, nevertheless, in the nervous sentiment of the correspondence. Kirkland seemed in the London letter to have worked out his dilemma and to have accepted his hard lot: "I wish I could tell you how happy I feel at this moment in thinking of you . . . whom, if Providence spares me, I shall see in four months at the farthest, and I hope, somewhat sooner." [18] As for Caroline, "I hope you will leave England the first of August if possible. We shall be all impatience—we did I say? Who will know what impatience is but your C." [19] William Kirkland arrived in Clinton in late August.

III   *The Western Experiment*

After the young people were married in mid-winter, January 10, 1828, they soon moved to Geneva, New York, where they started a girls' school in which they both taught. The school was not a really successful venture. Yet Kirkland's education and his astute mind were an inspiration to his wife; serious-minded young people, they had a common interest in education[20] and an earnest wish to see their pupils do well. In spite of their devotion and energy, Kirkland's deafness must have been a hindrance to them in conducting the school. Frustrations at the school were partially offset by domestic good fortunes; four children were born in Geneva—three daughters and a son Joseph who was to make his mark in American literature a generation later.[21] One of the daughters died in infancy.

In the spring of 1835 the Kirklands, like many of their neighbors in upstate New York, moved to the West. Opportunities on the frontier had often been described by new arrivals there in glittering phrases, and the crude living conditions and hard work which settlers experienced there had been so glossed over with romantic coloring that even alert and intelligent people like the Kirklands were deceived. The "reasonable prospect of a comfortable subsistence," which had eluded them in Geneva, seemed more promising in the West. Kirkland wanted to become a successful pioneer, hoping eventually to buy land on the Michigan frontier and to found a settlement. But money for such speculation was needed first, and to get it he accepted the principalship of the Detroit Female Seminary—which parents, anxious that good schools go with them to the West,[22] had recently established. A prospectus of the school appeared in a Detroit paper, announcing the opening of the new term under Kirkland's administration[23] and outlining the course of study the principal would offer.

Careful instruction in the solid and more generally useful branches will form the basis of his plan. . . . The ornamental branches will form the next objects of attention, and everything will be done to secure to the pupil as far as practicable, a solid, enlarged, and finished education.

Besides more intellectual culture, the formation of habits of quiet, method and industry will receive unceasing care. The inculcation of solemn principles of just views of life and doings, and the improvement of the affections will be regarded as an important duty.[24]

Kirkland's tenureship with the school commenced in auspicious times, for the Kirklands in their first year in Detroit found the city's population increasing daily with the arrival of emigrants from the East, many of them taking the route they themselves had followed: the Erie Canal to Buffalo, and then a lake steamer to Michigan. During the spring and summer of 1836 the city was jammed with emigrants—more than a thousand a day, it was reported. Some remained permanently in the growing city which could absorb many artisans and professional men in its expanding economy; others passed through the city and pushed farther to the West to settle in the wilderness. People living in the Michigan settlements anticipated the territory's becoming a state, and the steady flow of emigrants who swelled the population made it a reality the following year.

These were the years of the great Michigan land boom; and Kirkland, like so many other emigrants, began buying land—a few acres at first, but more and more as the months passed. He was, therefore, another of that host of speculators whom Mrs. Kirkland described later in *Western Clearings:* "[they] came to buy land,—not to clear and plough, but as men buy a lottery ticket or dig for gold—in the hope of unreasonable and unearned profits . . . strong in the faith of the boundless treasures which were to reward their perserverance." [25] By the end of the year, Kirkland had amassed eight hundred acres of land in his own name in what is now Livingston County, sixty miles northwest of Detroit; and, with his father's holdings, he now controlled over thirteen hundred acres of Michigan woodland and swamp.[26] Kirkland's wish—as he had dreamed about it in Geneva—was somewhat nearer reality: he had the land, and he would lay out a set-

tlement. He gave up the principalship of the seminary and turned
his energy to building the town called Pinckney. A plat of two
hundred acres was laid out, the village was roughly planned, and
the building of a mill was begun. The prospectus of the new village was circulated in the local papers in 1836 to encourage settlers:

> The village of Pinckney is situated in the southern part of Liv-
> ingston County, on Portage Creek, two miles from its entrance
> into Portage Lake. It is in the midst of one of the finest and best
> settled agricultural districts in the State, and is already the natural
> center of business for not less than two hundred or three hundred
> families. A Flouring-Mill is now in operation, which has just been
> constructed at a cost of from Seven to Eight Thousand Dollars,
> and there is no mill nearer than ten miles, and in some directions
> it will command the business for twenty miles. A good Temper-
> ance Tavern and Store have also been erected, and other buildings
> are in progress. A healthier spot is not to be found in Michigan.
> The State Road from Saganaw to the Chicago R^d at Clinton
> passes through this place, and the Grand River and Allegan
> State Road is expected to intersect the former at this point. The
> lots are 66 feet in front by 132 feet in depth. The streets are four
> rods in width, and the Public Square is sixteen rods square.[27]

The Kirkland family which moved to the frontier village in the
fall of 1837 included the parents and four youngsters ranging in
age from eleven years to six months. Another girl and boy had
been born to the Kirklands in Detroit; but, on the day of the birth
of the youngest child, an older child Sarah had fallen to her death
from a third-story window of the seminary. Mrs. Stansbury, who
had come to the West to live with her daughter and son-in-law,
had died in the spring of 1837. A seventh child, who lived only a
year, was to be born in Pinckney.[28] But sorrow could not be shown
openly on the frontier where it was such a common denominator.
In this respect at least Mrs. Kirkland was a pioneer woman already hardened to reality. Other harsh realities of frontier life she
bore stoically, resourcefully—many apparently with ready wit, as
one may see in A New Home. During the next six years in Pinckney, while her husband engaged in building the town and in additional land speculations, which she regarded with some humor,
she occupied herself with her frontier home, her children, her

neighbors, and with writing two books about her experiences: *A New Home—Who'll Follow?* (1839) and *Forest Life* (1842).[29]

Michigan proved, however, not to be the land of "boundless treasures." Nor was it the place for Kirkland to acquire "unreasonable and unearned profits" although many men with less principle, or more ignorance, did. Settlement promoters and land agents were out for the quick dollar. Kirkland was swindled by the land agent whom he had hired to lay out his settlement, and other kinds of graft were practiced.

> . . . when [the] speculators in land found that the glamor had departed . . . [when] poverty seem[ed] riches, and idleness industry, and fraud enterprise [Mrs. Kirkland recalled], some of these cunning magicians set themselves about concocting a new species of gramarye, by means of which the millions of acres of wild land which were left on their hands might be turned into *bona fide* cash—paper money at least. . . . The "General Banking Law" of enviable notoriety, which allowed any dozen of men who could pledge real estate to a nominal amount, to assume the power of making money of rags; this was the magic cauldron, whose powers were destined to transmute these acres of wood and meadow into splendid metropolitan residences. . . . It was only "bubble-bubble," and burr-oaks were turned into marble tables, tall tamaracks into draperied bedsteads, lakes into looking-glasses, and huge expanses of wet marsh into velvet couches. . . .[30]

The wild-cat banks sprang into villages overnight and just as abruptly vanished, issuing paper money which was soon discovered to be worthless and causing the settlers untold economic hardships. "How many settlers," Mrs. Kirkland wrote, "who came in from the deep woods many miles distant where no grain had yet grown, after travelling perhaps two or three days and nights, with a half-starved ox-team, and living on a few crusts by the way, were told when they offered their splendid-looking banknotes, their hard-earned all, for the flour which was to be the sole food of wife and babes through the long winter, that these hoarded treasures were valueless as the ragged paper which wrapped them!" [31] The Kirklands, like so many of their neighbors, were poorer than they had been before commencing their wilderness venture. And on their minds weighed the fact, too, that they had been responsible for getting many people to put their money into Michigan land, into William Kirkland and Company. They were openly disillusioned by their frontier experiment.

IV   *The Years in New York*

Because of their disappointment with the frontier experiment, the Kirklands decided to leave Michigan; they returned to New York City in 1843. They had missed the cultivation of the East, the association with alert minds.[32] Kirkland's interest had shifted from land speculation to the popular news media of the 1840's; Edgar Allan Poe recalled that Kirkland was highly regarded as a magazine writer and newspaper editor: what he wrote was "entitled to respect for its simplicity and evidence of scholarship and research." [33] He contributed essays to a number of periodicals, *Godey's* and the *Democratic Review* among them; and one article in particular—"The West, the Paradise of the Poor," which appeared in the *Democratic Review*—suggested other reasons for the Kirklands' leaving the West: they and the older children were already absorbing the stamp of the frontier. "Of the half-dozen families within the circle of our observation," he declared, "who came to the wilds with a larger share of intelligence and refinement than is possessed by the settlers generally, there is not one that is not degenerating in manners and mental habits; not one (we say it with sorrow) where the children are not inferior to the parents, or in fact, where they are materially above the uninstructed mass around them. The very atmosphere of society is averse to mental culture, and all refinement is so systematically as well as practically decried, as to have fallen into absolute discredit." [34] By 1846, the year of his premature death, Kirkland was editor of the New York *Evening Mirror* and co-editor with the Reverend Henry W. Bellows of the *Christian Inquirer*—a weekly Unitarian newssheet.[35]

And Mrs. Kirkland discovered that, like her grandfather, she enjoyed writing. "People write," she observed, "because they cannot help it." Remembering the furor she had caused by some of the comments about her neighbors in *A New Home*, she went on to say: "The heart longs for sympathy, and when it cannot be found close at hand, will seek it the world over. We never tell our thoughts but with the hope of an echo in the thoughts of others. We set forth in the most attractive guise the treasures of our fancy, because we hope to warm into life imaginations like our own. If the desire for sympathy could lie dormant for a time, there would be no more new books, and we should find leisure to read those already written." [36] She had begun to receive a little income from *A New Home,* and she had also been able to place her regional sketches and essays in a number of magazines: *Knickerbocker's,* the *Boston Miscellany, Graham's,* and the *Columbian.*

In December, 1840, Carey and Hart in Philadelphia had requested an article for *The Gift;* and she had complied with "The Bee-Tree." [37] She had written Rufus W. Griswold on several occasions about her willingness to forward articles for publication in *Graham's, "provided I accede to your terms."* Arranging *"terms"* agreeable to her, she meant to be paid more than the twenty-five dollars usually given to contributors; and she wanted the "liberty to make use of my contributions afterwards." [38] In the spring of 1843, she informed Griswold:

> I shall endeavor to send you very soon a very sentimental love story—or as near that as I can persuade myself to come—the trifle which accompanies this you must do as you think best with.— I should be glad if Mr. Graham would send me a draft for the amount due me.— I shall say nothing as to the price which I ought to receive for these intermediate pieces, relying on Mr. G.'s established reputation for liberality in these matters. . . . I wish to receive the $75 for "Conduct etc" and the compensation for the other pieces in one draft.[39]

She wrote deliberately, wishing to be unhurried; indeed, she told Carey and Hart a month later that she would not be able to send another story for the annual *Gift:* "[I] find your present demand somewhat astonishing. It will not be easy to furnish another long story for the same volume, and still preserve the air of variety so necessary for an Annual. . . . I am already engaged to furnish a story for [another] magazine." [40] Apparently her husband often acted as her literary adviser, making suggestions for revision and instructing her where to send the finished articles.[41] The idea of becoming a professional literary woman appealed to her; and, in the interims between preparing articles for magazine publication, she started work on a second book, *Forest Life.*[42]

In *A New Home* she had said that "one must come 'west' in order to learn a little of every thing." [43] One "thing" she learned was that her candid observations about life in the West had aroused the resentment of her neighbors. Remembering these cries of protest raised over *A New Home,* she no longer concentrated on life in one village but wrote in *Forest Life* about conditions generally along the Michigan frontier. The broader "arrangement of . . . materials," Mrs. Kirkland declared in the opening pages of *Forest Life,* would suggest more accurately the "moderate" or general characteristics of Western living.[44] Instead of informal portraits of neighbors and intimate remarks about local manners—matters which had made *A New Home* so delightful to read—she drew in *Forest Life* only character types and limited her observations to general discussions of frontier traits. In this broader view where the commonplaces of Western life—the "new-country customs and ways of thinking" [45]—were dealt with abundantly, Mrs. Kirkland anticipated the approach that the regionalists adopted in the latter decades of the nineteenth century when they patiently described ways of American life.

When the Kirklands returned to New York City, they both settled comfortably into quasi-literary work. For a time, they conducted a school,[46] perhaps fearful that their writing would not support them.[47] In the fall of 1846, Kirkland died, apparently by drowning—his body being recovered from the Hudson River near Fishkill, New York, where he had been visiting his son Joseph, who was in school. It was assumed that he fell from the dock in his haste to get on board the steamboat which was just pulling away from the landing. It was dusk; and, being near-sighted and deaf, he probably misjudged the distance he had to leap between the dock and the boat deck, fell into the river, and was swept under water by the eddying currents the engines were making. The noise of the engines prevented passengers on board from hearing a cry for help.[48]

For the remaining years of her life, Mrs. Kirkland alternated between teaching and writing. The responsibility of supporting and educating four children was solely her own, except for the teen-aged jobs Elizabeth and Joseph could perform. She conducted several girls' schools herself and was associated as a teacher with several others. After the publication of *Western Clearings* in the year of her husband's death, she edited for eighteen months, beginning in 1847, a new literary magazine of real merit, *The Union Magazine of Literature and Art.*

As an editor, she looked for realism in the fiction she read for publication: "Nine-tenths of the magazine stories, so popular among us, have nothing to do with this life," she declared; "and fiction which has no relation to what has been, or what is to be, must be both vapid and valueless." Mindful of the women readers, mindful too of the fact that she was woman and mother, she also believed that it was a solemn duty of "those who write for the public . . . to aim at raising the standard of taste, and improving, in every possible way, the powers of those who read. Nobody has a right, morally speaking, to send forth in print that which has no good aim." [49]

Mrs. Kirkland was associated with the magazine for a number of years—as an editor, as a contributor, and as an agent for new talent; she wrote Western sketches, editorials, reviews of books, accounts of her journeys through Europe (first in 1848 and again in 1850), and essays about education, manners, and morals which were intended primarily for women readers. Of special interest to her perhaps were little essays on the pretensions of "literary women" and the frustrations of "lion-hunting." [50] She also did piece work for her New York friends William Cullen Bryant, Evert A. and George L. Duyckinck, and Nathaniel Parker Willis; contributed to her husband's Unitarian paper, the *Christian Inquirer;* and wrote prefaces for books, among them one for Mrs. Mary Eastman's *Dahcotah* (1849).

Her life was an active one, yet the death of her husband was a sore affliction. "I am left a life of struggle and anxiety," she wrote a correspondent. "My children are to be educated and provided for—on my own and their earnings principally— But these are as nothing. . . . My loss is all—I depended, heart and soul, on my husband—I feel unfit to walk alone—and I have unhappily not learned to depend, practically and habitually, on God, for the same kind of support and counsel." [51] Yet Mrs. Kirkland was not the kind of woman to bemoan her lot; for purpose, determination, and acceptance were the very fabric of the life she had lived. As so many passages in her instructive essays reveal, she never doubted that God was in His Heaven, or that God was good. Like William Kirkland, she did not believe in the older faith of his New England predecessors; her sympathies, like his, were with Unitarianism. To her, it was better to work and pray, not watch and pray; for God helped those who first helped themselves. And her New

York friends Bryant, the Duyckincks, and Willis—later Bayard Taylor and Charles F. Briggs—often came to her aid by giving her assignments.

It was probably the publishers of the *Union* who paid a large share of the expense of the first trip to Europe, although she traveled with her friends, the Reverend and Mrs. Henry W. Bellows. The tour through Europe resulted in a two-volume book on her travels: *Holidays Abroad; or Europe from the West* (1849)—"a work of nice observations of men and manners," Bryant recalled, "and full of entertainment." [52] A number of these "letters," the ones on English life and manners particularly, had previously appeared in the *Union*. In 1852 she published *The Evening Book or, Fireside Talk on Morals and Manners, with Sketches of Western Life*, and in 1853 a companion volume, *A Book for the Home Circle; or, Familiar Thoughts on Various Topics, Literary, Moral and Social* (these "talks" and "sketches" had been printed in the *Union* and in the other magazines to which she contributed): "sensible essays on topics of interest in every day society," wrote the Duyckincks.[53] Another miscellany appeared in 1854, *Autumn Hours, and Fireside Reading*. Such gift books were very well liked by the women of her day, and Mrs. Kirkland was one of the more popular editors. She continued to edit them because the readers, in her words, had "shown themselves kindly willing to be pleased." [54]

After *The Helping Hand,* a plea for rehabilitation of women convicts, which was not published until 1853, she was commissioned by Putnam's to supply the literary material for *The Book of Home Beauty* (1852)—an elaborate gift book for the Christmas trade containing twelve engraved portraits of women who were prominent in New York society. "The literary part of a Book of Beauty,—secondary, of course, to the artistic,—should be merely a slight web of kindred thoughts," Mrs. Kirkland wrote tastefully in a preface; "all pleasant and good thoughts being, to our thinking, akin to Beauty." [55] The "slight web of kindred thoughts"— called "Search after Pleasure"—was so well thought of apparently that it was reprinted in *Autumn Hours,* a much cheaper book for women readers.

For her "young friends, known and unknown," she wrote *Personal Memoirs of George Washington* (1857), a conventional biography; and also edited two collections of sentimental, instructive verse: *Garden Walks with the Poets* (1852) and *The School-Girl's Garland* (1864). She had edited in 1846, also for young people, a volume of selections from one of her favorite poets, Edmund Spenser: "an humble attempt to introduce [the poet] to common American readers . . . intended for a reading book for the higher classes in schools." [56]

Mrs. Kirkland was well known in New York social and literary circles at the mid-century, according to Poe's tribute in "The Literati of New York City." Her personal manner, Poe thought, was an echo of her literary one: she was frank, firm yet cordial, "converse[d] with remarkable accuracy as well as fluency; [was] brilliantly witty, and now and then not a little sarcastic." There was "a general amiability" in her manner: "her whole countenance beam[ed] with benevolence and intellect." [57] Her own home was a literary salon as was that of her friend Mrs. Anne Lynch Botta. Mrs. Kirkland's letters and briefly penned invitations to people like Mrs. Lydia Maria Child, Mrs. Anna Cora Mowatt, Miss Catharine Maria Sedgwick, Mrs. Lydia Huntley Sigourney, and Mrs. Anne Sophia Stephens (her literary friends who also edited or wrote for women's magazines); to Bryant, the Duyckincks, Poe, Taylor, and Willis indicated her interest in evenings given over to stimulating—if not always intellectual—discussions. On one occasion at least her home was opened for a musicale for the benefit of the poor women of the city.[58] And once Ralph Waldo Emerson came to call.[59]

But the schedule Mrs. Kirkland set for herself during these years in New York—the editing and the writing and the literary evenings with friends—ended abruptly, as the normal routine did for many Americans in the 1860's, with the coming of the war. The tempo of city life quickened, and New York reflected the new urgency as its citizens responded to the demands of the war. The city "threw off the costumes of peace with indifferent hand," Walt Whitman proclaimed in *Drum-Taps*, ". . . [its] soft opera-music changed, and the drum and fife were heard in their stead" with "young men falling in and arming," answering the government's calls for volunteers. An ardent supporter of the Union, Mrs. Kirkland supplied a large number of patriotic pieces for the magazines and newssheets, devoted time and energy to various war-related programs and benefits, and saw her son Joseph become an officer in the Union army. She even corrected her son's articles for *The*

Continental Magazine, when his inclination or his duties in the field prevented him from making his own revisions.[60] She also persuaded her friends, among them Mrs. Child, to contribute articles to *The Prairie Chicken,* the newspaper her son edited for a year beginning in October, 1864—one of many similar papers issued in the country for the benefit of the United States Sanitary Commission. Proceeds from the sales of such papers went to a general fund used for the benefit of wounded soldiers and sailors. Joseph Kirkland published posthumously three articles by his mother in *The Prairie Chicken.* One of them, "Essay on Works of Fiction: Written as a Preface to an Unpublished Novel," indicated that Mrs. Kirkland was apparently planning before her death a full-length piece of fiction.

When the Metropolitan Fair was held in New York in the spring of 1864 for the benefit of the Sanitary Commission, Mrs. Kirkland took an active part in its organization and management —tireless, it seemed, in her energy and dedication. She attended the opening of the fair on Monday, April 4, wrote Bryant in an obituary notice; was active with her committee of ladies in the hall devoted to arranging arms and trophies on Tuesday; was seized with apoplexy on Wednesday morning, April 6, 1864, and died before medical aid could be given.[61]

CHAPTER 2

A New Home—Who'll Follow?

Our friends in the "settlements" have expressed so much interest in such of our letters to them, as happened to convey an account of the peculiar features of western life, and have asked so many curious questions, touching particulars which we had not thought worthy of mention, that I have been for some time past contemplating the possibility of something like a detailed account of our experiences . . . a veracious history of actual occurrences, an unvarnished transcript of real characters. . . .

The reader who has patience to go with me to the close of my desultory sketches, must expect nothing beyond a meandering recital of common-place occurrences—mere gossip about everyday people, little enhanced in value by any fancy or ingenuity of the writer; in short, a very ordinary pen-drawing; which, deriving no interest from coloring, can be valuable only for its truth.

—*A New Home*

M RS. KIRKLAND claimed for *A New Home*, the first book of Western sketches of life and manners, "a general truth of outline"; in fact, she declared in the preface, "I felt somewhat tempted to set forth my little book as being entirely, what it is very nearly—a sort of 'Emigrant's guide'. . . ." She did admit that there were in the narrative "glosses, and colorings, and lights, if not shadows," for which she alone was accountable; but, in a way that was to be characteristic of her nimble mind, she concluded: "whatever is quite unnatural, or absolutely incredible . . . is to be received as literally true. It is only in the common-place parts . . . that I have any leasing-making to answer for." [1]

What Mrs. Kirkland (she used the pen name Mrs. Mary Clavers) had to say in the following pages was meant in the spirit in which it was written—a forthright history primarily of her "adventures" in the raw Michigan wilderness of the 1830's, humorous comments about her neighbors, her family *and* herself which sometimes identified the "incredible" in their daily lives, in their opinions, habits, and pretensions.[2] For she had a cheerful disposition and the happy faculty of seeing the ridiculous or the ludicrous in a situation. She could as easily laugh at her own folly of walking through a swamp in paper-soled shoes as she could find amusement in her neighbor "Elovees" Fidler's carrying around a little album in the pocket of a blue silk apron, "ever ready to secure a passing thought or an elegant quotation."

She could also laugh at her own arrival in Pinckney (she called the village Montacute in the book)[3] with house plants, her greyhound D'Orsay, a basket of live chickens, and "an enormous square box crammed with articles which we then in our greenness considered indispensable" as she could be amused at the "unnatural" formality of the schoolmistress Cleory Jenkins, who had come to call dressed in the height of wilderness fashion yet smoking her pipe "with the greatest gusto, turning ever and anon to spit at the hearth." What some of the neighbors did not realize was that Mrs. Kirkland's sense of the human comedy allowed her to regard her own behavior as being as amusing as theirs; she could smile at herself just as she smiled at them. Yet *A New Home*—in spite of its good-natured humor—was an intensely personal narrative, the frank reactions of a genteel woman to the primitiveness of frontier society.

The charge was later made by her neighbors in Pinckney that Mrs. Kirkland's interest in *A New Home* with what might be called social improprieties proved that she had arrived in the wilderness with the polite conventions common enough in a more sophisticated society and that she had spent much of her time noting the gaucheries of wilderness conduct which would make good reading in the parlors of her friends in the East. There was truth in the charge that she was a gentlewoman writing about the lowbrow manners of her frontier neighbors,[4] as she herself implied in the first sentence of the narrative. But she was able to recognize also her own "incredibilities," the folly of holding such notions and such possessions in a frontier community: she readily admitted that her lovely china tureen would make a good chamber pot, as her neighbor Mr. Jennings advised; that her large mahogany cupboard, too big for the small log cabin, would make a good corn crib, as the "hired" girl indicated; that her delicate japanned tables would be more useful as kindling than as ornaments set out upon the uneven wooden floor. When it came to "reconciling" fashionable opinions of propriety or good taste to backwoods conditions, she was willing to confess that the practical advantages outweighed the fanciful notions she had brought with her to the West. The Michigan wilderness was no place to nourish fashionable sentiments.

I   *The West as American Writers Saw It*

In fact, she was equally quick to acknowledge the error of other romantic notions she had held. "When I first 'penetrated the interior,' (to use an indigenous phrase) all I knew of the wilds was from [Charles Fenno] Hoffman's tour or Captain [James] Hall's 'graphic' delineations: I had some floating idea of 'driving a barouche-and-four anywhere through the oak-openings'. . . . I confess, these pictures, touched by the glowing pencil of fancy, gave me but incorrect notions of a real journey through Michigan." [5] Her "real" experience in backwoods travel was made dramatically clear when she and her husband encountered their first mudhole:

> I had just indulged in something like a yawn, and wished that I could see our hotel. At the word, my [husband's] face assumed rather a comical expression, and I was preparing to inquire somewhat testily what there was so laughable—I was getting tired and cross, reader—when down came our good horse to the very chin in a bog-hole, green as Erin on the top, but giving way on a touch, and seeming deep enough to have engulphed us entirely. . . . Down came the horse—and this was not all—down came the driver; and I could not do less than follow, though at a little distance—our good steed kicking and floundering—covering us with hieroglyphics, which would be readily deciphered by any Wolverine we should meet, though perchance strange to the eyes of our friends at home.[6]

It was not long before Mrs. Kirkland realized that what she had read about the primitive life was very different from what she found it to be. Her home in Michigan was never to be as handsome a framed house with space for the family and for entertaining as she had fondly hoped:

> The circumstances of living all summer, in the same apartment with a cooking fire, I had never happened to see alluded to in

any of the elegant sketches of western life which had fallen under
my notice. It was not until I actually became the inmate of a log
dwelling in the wilds, that I realized fully what "living all in one
room" meant. The sleeping apparatus for the children and the
sociable Angeline, were in the loft; but my own bed, with its cunning fence of curtains; my bureau, with its "Alps on Alps" of
boxes and books; my entire cooking array; my center-table, which
bore, sad change! the remains of today's dinner, and the prepara-
tions for to-morrow, all covered mysteriously under a large cloth,
the only refuge from the mice: these and ten thousand other
things, which a summer's day would not suffice me to enumerate,
cumbered this one single apartment; and to crown the whole was
the inextinguishable fire, which I had entirely forgotten when I
magnanimously preferred living in a log-house, to remaining in
Detroit till a house could be erected. I had . . . dwelt with delight on Chateaubriand's Atala, where no such vulgar inconven-
ience is once hinted at; and my floating visions of a home in the
woods were full of important omissions, and always in a Floridian
clime, where fruits serve for *vivers*.[7]

Native authors, when writing about the West, as Mrs. Kirkland
and many of her contemporaries who migrated to the frontier discovered, wrote of the area largely in terms of romance or adventure—the approach which had been employed by Washington
Irving in *A Tour on the Prairies* (1835), by Timothy Flint in
George Mason, the Young Backwoodsman (1829), by Robert
Montgomery Bird in *Nick of the Woods* (1837), even by James
Hall in a number of "legends" about the West. As Percy H. Boynton has indicated, "The rivalry between fact and sentiment is
ceaseless in the literature of the frontier. . . . When the frontier
was still a reality, the temptation to idealize it was strongest. It
was a land of hope and promise, a place of escape from the
drudgery of here and now . . . [and] the first writer, or the early
writer, on the frontier was bound by this preconception."[8]

In preparing for the journey to Michigan (or sometime after
her arrival there), Mrs. Kirkland apparently read accounts of
writers' impressions of the West, specifically Hoffman's tour and
Hall's "graphic" descriptions. Hoffman's overland journey to
Cleveland, the trip by lake steamer to Detroit, the month's tour on
horseback through the Michigan backwoods took him over much
the same route which the Kirklands traveled less than a year later.
Perhaps the "tolerably smooth passage" Hoffman enjoyed on the

lake steamer was similar to theirs; and his first impression of Detroit—sprawled over "an elevated piece of table-land" with "spacious street[s]" lined only with stark wooden "dwelling-houses"
somewhat hastily erected following the "great fire twenty years
since"—was doubtless theirs: "the appearance of the place is any
thing but what you would expect from a town founded in the
same year as Philadelphia." [9] Once in the hinterland, however,
Hoffman allowed a preconceived vision of the West to direct his
pen:

> What a country this is. Into land like this, which is comparatively
> undervalued by those seeking to settle on the prairie, a man can
> run his plough without felling a tree; and, planting a hundred
> acres, where he would clear but ten in the unsettled districts of
> New York, raise his twenty-five bushels of wheat an acre in the
> very first season. "How is the soil here, sir?" I said to a farmer
> whose broad fields, though but a year under cultivation, looked
> as if they had been tilled for ten. "A pretty good gravelly loam
> of eighteen inches; but I think some of moving off to Kalamazoo,
> where they have it *four feet deep, and so fat that it will grease
> your fingers.*" Railroads and canals will make one broad garden
> of Michigan. . . . The absence of stumps in the land under cul-
> tivation, and the open groves adjacent, give a smiling openness to
> the landscape which, with myriads of wild flowers that brighten
> the woods in their season, must make the aspect of the country
> perfectly delightful.[10]

"The ease with which a man can here support a family as a
farmer," he speculated, "induces a great many persons of all pro-
fessions . . . to abandon their former pursuits and become tillers
of the soil. The alteration of life, I should judge by the contentment I every where witness, is almost always for the better." And
he marveled at the "great many English emigrants . . . who, I
am told, are successfully introducing here the use of live hedges
instead of fences in farming." [11]

The fact that low-lying, marshy lands were often a hazard to
health was ignored by the romantic observer.[12] Some emigrants,
Hoffman admitted, "did allow the existence of bilious fevers and
fever and ague, in every part of the country; but they spoke of
passing through these diseases as merely a slight process of *accli-
mating*, which, in the general health of the country, was hardly to

be considered. They asserted, too, what I have beforehand heard stated by more than one physician in the territory, that Michigan is exempt from many of the diseases most fatal to life in the East." [13] Too often Hoffman reported what he *heard,* not what he saw (for his was a mid-winter tour). And too often the temptation to romanticize was stronger than the demand to write realistically. The West was indeed a land of hope and promise for those who worked; but it was not a place to escape the drudgery of hard labor, like felling trees and clearing stumps from the land. Hoffman was a traveler, a visitor, who saw only casually the life of the Western settler.

The misty vision of the traveler deceived Irving as well, when he toured the American West after years of absorbing the sights and sounds of Europe. "It seems to me," he descried in *A Tour on the Prairies,* "as if these beautiful regions answer literally to the description of the land of promise, 'a land flowing with milk and honey'; for the rich pasturage of the prairies is calculated to sustain herds of cattle as countless as the sands upon the sea-shore, while the flowers with which they are enamelled render them a very paradise for the nectar-seeking bee." [14] Enthralled by the grandeur of the scenes he was witnessing, he expressed sentiments which at least some of his readers—among them, prospective emigrants to the West—felt:

> Such is the glorious independence of men in a savage state. This youth [one of the hunting party], with his rifle, his blanket, and his horse, was ready at a moment's warning to rove the world; he carried all his worldly effects with him, and in the absence of artificial wants, possessed the great secret of personal freedom. We of society are slaves, not so much to others as to ourselves; our superfluities are the chains that bind us, impeding every movement of our bodies and thwarting every impulse of our souls. Such, at least, were my speculations at the time. . . . [15]

A primitivist for the moment, Irving could "lay on the grass under the trees, and [build] castles in the clouds, and [indulge] in the very luxury of rural repose . . . scarcely conceiv[ing] a kind of life more calculated to put both mind and body in a healthful tone." [16]

The sights and sounds of the wilderness, the frontiersmen and the Indians—Irving saw, however, through European eyes. And,

as he made entries in his memorandum book, he made them remembering what he had seen in Europe, drawing analogies his
European readers would be familiar with. The Osages—"stately
fellows . . . [with] fine Roman countenances . . . look[ing]
like so many noble bronze figures"—wore closely-cropped hair
"excepting a bristling ridge on the top," which he compared to the
crest of a helmet. The Creeks, on the other hand, were gaily
dressed "in calico hunting-shirts of various brilliant colors, deco-
rated with bright fringes, and belted with broad girdles, embroi-
dered with beads. . . ." Irving needed not to add that they reminded him—as they would his knowledgeable reader—of the
colorfully dressed gypsies he had seen on the highways of Spain. A
half-breed, whose manner Irving confessed he did not like, had
features "shaped not unlike those of Napoleon, but sharpened up,
with high Indian cheek bones." Another companion on the
tour—a "raw-boned, hard-winking, hard-riding knight-errant of
the frontier"—reminded him of the description of the hero of La
Mancha.[17] Echoes of the remembered past filled the memorandum
book and spilled out in the pages of the *Tour:*

> We were overshadowed by lofty trees, with straight, smooth
> trunks, like stately columns [Irving wrote further on]; and as the
> glancing rays of the sun shone through the transparent leaves,
> tinted with the many-colored hues of autumn, I was reminded of
> the effect of sunshine among the stained windows and clustering
> columns of a Gothic cathedral. Indeed there is a grandeur and
> solemnity in our spacious forests of the West, that awaken in me
> the same feeling I have experienced in those vast and venerable
> piles, and the sound of the wind sweeping through them, supplies
> occasionally the deep breathing of the organ.[18]

Irving wrote for his readers the brand of sentimentalized romance
to which they had become accustomed; like so many of his contemporaries who were writing about the West, Irving—in the
words of Percy H. Boynton—"set his imagination in a fertile
land," washing a virgin wilderness in a soft autumnal glow. Such
an approach was "a salable formula for the writer of popular romance," [19] but it was not a transcript of Western experience.

Good writing about the frontier had to come from men and
women who lived there and who knew it firsthand; and it was
somewhat surprising that the authors who had lived in the wil-

derness still perpetuated the myth. Flint's *George Mason, the Young Backwoodsman* could have been a contribution to nascent American fiction, for the details of the novel were drawn from the author's youthful experiences in the West. Yet the "honest roots" (the phrase is Alexander Cowie's)[20] were too soon entangled in a sentimental tale—as sophomoric as Mrs. Kirkland's homilies written later for the women's magazines. There was little realism in the story, except the descriptions of nature. Although Bird exploded the myth of the noble savage in his relentless treatment of the Indian in *Nick of the Woods,* he did make good capital of the myth of the stalwart backwoodsman, relying on his readers' knowledge of the glamorous exploits of men like Daniel Boone and Davy Crockett. Mrs. Kirkland, if she read the novel, might have been amused, and instructed, by the comic talk of Ralph Stackpole and the Bruces; and she might have compared speculation in public lands in Kentucky with the land fever in Michigan. But Bird's novel was also largely a copybook romance with enough Gothic sensationalism to whet the popular taste.

Hall seemed through personal experience the best equipped to write realistically about the West, having made the region his home for many years. In a prolific number of essays, sketches, and tales, he delineated the backwoods character types: hunters and farmers, itinerant preachers, sturdy pioneer women, faith-healers, jacks-of-all-trades, even French riverboatmen and English mercantile clerks who had turned farmers. He had the historian's eye for materials rich in human interest, but even he could not forbear sentiment and picturesqueness in what was mainly a romantic vision of the West. Cooper and Scott were obviously not models to follow, if an author intended to write with fidelity; but they were models to follow if one wished to write for the popular taste. Perhaps Hall compromised ability for popularity and was content, therefore, with sketching general traits of basically noble Western character and with perpetuating a mighty vision of the West.

It is true [he wrote in *Legends of the West*], that our people had some vague notions of their own importance, and would sometimes talk of their *birth-rights* and their *future greatness,* in a strain that would make a stranger stare. Accustomed to the contemplation of great mountains, long rivers, and boundless plains, the majestic features of their country swelled their ideas, and gave a tinge of romance to their conceptions. The immense cotton-

woods and sycamores that overhung their rivers, the huge alligator
that bellowed in the stream and the great mammoth bones im-
bedded in their swamps became familiar standards of comparison;
while their long journeys over boundless plains teeming with the
products of nature, gave them exalted notions of the magnificence
of their country. One would have thought they were speaking in
parables, who heard them describing the old thirteen states as a
mere appendage of the future republic—a speck on the map of
the United States—a sort of out-lot with a cotton field at one end,
and a manufactory of wooden clocks at the other; yet they were
in sober earnest.[21]

Mrs. Kirkland did observe the Westerner's feeling of grandiose
self-importance—a detriment to his character, as she saw it; but
she could not accept Hall's romanticizing frontier life in stories his
readers were willing to believe. "I have been reading Judge Hall,"
she wrote Evert Duyckinck a few years later. "I confess with
something of a *Balaam-ish* feeling—hoping, perhaps to find him
dull—so that there might be no love lost between him and Mrs.
Clavers. . . . I cannot deny that the Judge is very agreeable . . .
altho' he saw a different West from any that ever met my
view." [22] What she might have found unaccountably "dull"—so-
porific, at any rate—were the tales and sketches overcharged with
sentiment or the homilies she herself was occasionally injecting in
her Western material. " 'Graphic' delineations" of the West, Mrs.
Kirkland satirically noted, they were not.

II   *Mrs. Kirkland's "Transcript of Reality"*

Frontiersmen, Mrs. Kirkland discovered, were in reality far removed from a state of innocence. Life in the woods had not made
them essentially noble, had in fact reduced many of them to a
"savage state" Irving had little imagined. Men on the border were
showing some pretty ignoble traits that were all the more apparent because of the land boom in Michigan. There was truth in the
complaint of Cooper's trapper who could not escape "the sound of
axes, and the crash of falling trees." The conquest of the wilderness, as Mrs. Kirkland reacted to it, was a rather shabby business,
one that was destructive and wasteful of resources, human and
natural. The "one broad garden" Hoffman had prophesied Michigan would become was often sprouting seeds of greed, envy, and
discontent.[23]

Men were greedy to make fortunes during the land boom in the
easiest way possible: if not with lumber and skins, then through
land speculation and chicanery. Land promoters engaged auc-
tioneers to sell their marsh areas in the hinterland on the Detroit
market as valuable lots in virgin woods.

> [Such] an auctioneer was . . . a man of genius [Mrs. Kirk-
> land observed], of ready invention, of fluent speech; one who had
> seen something of the world, and above all, one who must be so
> thoroughly acquainted with the property, and so entirely con-
> vinced of its value, that he could vouch on his own personal *re-
> spectability*, for the truth of every statement. He must be able to
> exhibit certificates from—no matter whom—Tom-a-Nokes per-
> haps—but "residing on the spot"—and he must find men of straw
> to lead the first bids. . . . [I]t must have required some nerve to
> carry the matter through; to stand by, while the poor artizan, the
> journeyman mechanic, the stranger who had brought his little all
> to buy government land to bring up his young family upon, staked
> their poor means on strips of land which were at the moment a
> foot under water.[24]

The settlement promoters were often no more honest, offering
shares in their newly opened villages to unwary emigrants for
three hundred dollars apiece (with the chance of quadrupling
the investment in a month) and never mentioning "that the whole
had been purchased for four hundred dollars, just a week before . . . [in] Detroit." [25]

The "tricksy spirit" was everywhere manifest; Mrs. Kirkland
spoke not only as the impassioned observer but as an unwary victim. She and her husband had innocently traded two lots in
Pinckney at five hundred dollars each for one lot in a still newer
settlement at a thousand dollars. Inquiring later about the settlement, they were told, "There's nobody there." [26]

This quest for what Mrs. Kirkland called in *Western Clearings*
"unreasonable and unearned profits" at the expense of unsuspecting victims was a flagrant abuse of the Western wilderness. The
exploitation of the Michigan frontier often brought out the worst
in man; and, in her sketches, she did not sentimentalize the backwoodsman as Hall had. To her, such a settler was frequently a
creature bent on self-satisfaction, in spite of "intuitive" sympathies. She wrote later in *Forest Life*:

His character, his habits, his faults, his virtues, his points of pe-
culiarity, of superiority, of inferiority, are very striking, but it is
not easy to describe them concisely. He is a being at once calcu-
lating and impetuous—penurious and prodigal—indolent and la-
borious—rough and kindly—passionate and forgiving; vowing
revenge today; and tomorrow doing a kindness to his declared
enemy. He will make his wife a drudge without compunction;
but his old mother must have a warm corner, and the privilege of
knitting or doing nothing, as she chooses. He will, likely enough,
give his father a short answer if he attempts to interfere with the
ordering of business, but the old man will never lack any of his
accustomed comforts while his son is able to earn them. His
temper is hasty, and his sentiments are not very refined. . . .[27]

Actual residence in the West made her a realist; and, in her first
book about Western life, she cut through the romantic fabric of
the frontier myth and in the process brought a vigor and strength
to American writing too long marred by sentimentalism and high
adventure.

As significant as *A New Home* is to early American realism, it is
sometimes a satiric commentary on Western manners and on
traits of character by a witty, worldly woman who confessedly
looked at her material from an "outlander's" vantage point. In
time she would become somewhat Westernized, but in *A New
Home* she was often condescending in her attitude. She laughed
at herself, yet more often she was laughing at her neighbors. Mrs.
Jennings, who obliged Mrs. Kirkland by helping her settle the
house, had the annoying habit of drinking from the spout of the
pot any tea that was left, saying that it tasted better. If she didn't,
she told Mrs. Kirkland, she would have "the 'sterics so that she
wasn't able to do a chore." When she sat down with the family to
eat, she dipped her own spoon into every dish on the table; or
grabbing a ham hock in her hand, she cut out a chunk with her
knife, declining any aid from her astonished hostess. "I'll help
myself, I thank ye. I never want no waitin' on." [28]

The widow Mrs. Nippers was the next-door neighbor, whose
main occupation was furnishing the town with gossip. No man
could sneeze on his own doorstep; no child could be late for
school; no hen could lay an egg in the afternoon or a cow be
missing at milking time; nor could a young couple steal away for a
few minutes of innocent love-making in the woods that Mrs. Nip-

pers didn't know about it and tell anybody who would listen. She
organized the Montacute Female Beneficent Society—"the foun-
tain of village scandal," Mrs. Kirkland slyly noted, "the hot-bed
from which springs every root of bitterness . . . [where the]
talking sex of Montacute" engaged in lively conversation at the
weekly meetings:

> "Do you have any butter now?" "When are you going to raise
> your barn?" "Is your man a going to kill, this week?" "I ha'n't seen
> a bit of meat these six weeks." "Was you to meetin' last Sabbath?"
> "Has Miss White got any wool to sell?" "Do tell if you've been
> to Detroit!" "Are you out o' candles?" "Well I *should* think Sarah
> Teals wanted a new gown!" "I hope we shall have milk in a
> week or two," and so on.[29]

If Mrs. Kirkland was naïve enough to think that such comments would not be resented in Pinckney, she was mistaken. The
"slander" aroused great anger, as a contemporary account
recorded:

> . . . [the] sketch of a meeting of the female society . . .
> raised against [Mrs. Kirkland] a whirlwind of indignation among
> her Pinckney neighbors. In that sketch she drew her pen portraits,
> not too flattering of the inhabitants of the place, their oddities,
> bad manners and vulgarities. She had supposed that it was all
> concealed by calling the town Montacute and altering the names
> of the actors, and that no copies of the work would find their way
> to that remote settlement. But in this she was mistaken, and the
> result was that all the persons thus truthfully depicted, were
> exasperated almost to frenzy. One woman threatened to have her
> put under bonds, and the life of the Kirkland family in Pinckney
> thereafter was the reverse of agreeable.[30]

And a letter written by a New York State lawyer who traveled
in Michigan several years later revealed that the rancor, particularly among the women of Pinckney, still ran deep:

> I passed through Mrs. Kirkland's neighborhood on my last west-
> ern tour. She and her husband live at a little village called Pink-
> ney [*sic*] in Livingston County. . . . I found she was in bad
> odure with her neighbors. They had heard of her book, but had

not seen it. She keeps it out of Michigan. I was diverted at the spirit manifested by the ladies of the log cabin where I stopped to warm. They told me Mrs. Kirkland intended to point out real characters in her neighborhood, and slander them most scandalously. That [it] was well known who she meant, and she had better attend to her own family and let other people's alone. Not having seen the book, they are more convinced from what they hear that they are all satirized and scandalized by name, almost. They informed me she is writing another book this winter and hires a girl to wash her dishes. She should be more usefully employed. There is not the least benefit to mind or mortals in her writings.[31]

Although the comments about the "oddities" of her wilderness neighbors might well be amusing, a truly vexing social habit of Westerners for Mrs. Kirkland and her husband was the habit of borrowing: "Mother wants your sifter, and she says she guesses you can let her have some sugar and tea, 'cause you've got plenty.'" This excellent reason, "'cause you've got plenty," was sufficient for sharing with neighbors. Whoever came to Michigan with only a few worldly goods or personal possessions, Mrs. Kirkland declared, could through borrowing easily improve his holdings; and to have either money or household conveniences and not share them with neighbors was an unpardonable social sin. She recalled a farmer who lent a martingale to his neighbor; its route was then traced to four dwellings two miles apart, having been lent from one farmer to another without a word to the owner who sat at home, waiting, not very patiently, to commence his own journey. "Sieves, smoothing irons, and churns, run about as if they had legs; one brass kettle is enough for a whole neighborhood; and I could point to a cradle which has rocked half the babies in Montacute. For my own part, I have lent my broom, my thread, my tape, my spoons, my cat, my thimble, my scissors, my shawl, my shoes; and have been asked for my combs and brushes; and my husband, for his shaving apparatus and his pantaloons." [32]

Borrowing was carried on without the slightest conscience on the part of the borrower. When a neighbor learned that a friend or acquaintance had anything which might contribute to his convenience, he simply announced his needs and expected compliance with the demand. It was a well-thought-out system, William Kirkland observed in "The West, the Paradise of the Poor":

. . . we speak advisedly—we mean system, not practice. . . .
Its importance to the well-doing of him who comes into the woods
with nothing, is seen at a glance. Every neighborhood is, by this
plan, turned into a joint-stock association, the goods of each and
every member being, in some sense, common property. It differs
from other joint-stock companies in this: that the less anyone puts
in the more he takes out. No fee is required for admission into
this general loan company; mere residence confers its privileges,
as it does those of citizenship. The new-comer is occasionally
troubled with a little bashfulness about using his freedom, but he
soon shakes it off, and becomes as perfect in the art of borrowing
as those to whom it has become second nature. It requires but a
short time to get the run of needful articles, so as to know pretty
nearly where to find them when wanted, and then the work is
done.[33]

To the Kirklands, who had not set out for the West until they had
assured themselves that all their needs were provided for, such a
habit was outrageous and personally annoying. Moreover, neighbors in New York State had not practiced these expediencies.

III *Western Individualism*

What can be defined as regional in Mrs. Kirkland's Western
sketches is most clearly evident in *Forest Life* and in her later
magazine pieces; it is not so apparent in *A New Home,* where the
West was usually seen through the "outlander's" eyes and where
the reactions sometimes bore the mark of Mrs. Kirkland's precon-
victions. Yet her observations in *A New Home* about Western individualism—although personal in nature—suggested what she
was to recognize later: that individualism was an essential characteristic of the region. Her analysis grew out of comments about
her neighbors' habit of borrowing—a "system," she and her husband concluded, which was intimately associated with the concept of individualism—a concept at once admirable and censurable.

It manifested itself most importantly in the feeling of equality
the frontiersman held. On the one hand, the West offered the settler opportunity. "We had most awful hard times at first," one of
Mrs. Kirkland's neighbors told her. "Many's the day I've worked
from sunrise till dark in the fields gathering brush heaps and burning stumps. But that's all over now; and we've got four times as

much land as we ever should have owned in York State." [34]
Through backbreaking work the settler could improve his lot; it
was the realization of the American dream that St. Jean de
Crèvecoeur had written about in *Letters from an American
Farmer* (1782) and that Hoffman and Hall had so glowingly
described. The West was truly a paradise for the man, William
Kirkland wrote, "whose capital lies in his hands, and whose income is just what those hands can procure him, employed in the
roughest service which mother Earth exacts of her rudest sons.
For such a man the Western wilderness is a blooming field, and
. . . there is no fiction, in calling the West his home." [35] Such
individualism was appropriately a cherished American right, and
it often led to generosity; for a neighbor more fortunate gave more
freely to his friend who was down on his luck. "We do a great deal
more for each other . . . ," Kirkland was informed, "and we don't
think nothing of it neither." [36]

Nevertheless, the Kirklands believed, a kind of jaundiced, irrational behavior sometimes resulted from such individualism. Since
the West provided, in its natural resources, wood for the building
of the home, fuel for warmth, and land for the farmer's livelihood,
everyone wanted to be a landowner and to work much or little his
own plot of wilderness. This independence, or equality, having
been encouraged by the government which had given the settler
the opportunity to stake his own homestead, no man needed to
work for another; and those "who desire such services are obliged
to bid high for them," noted Kirkland, "in order to induce the
[freeholder] to defer for a while the satisfaction of working for
[himself]." The precious right of serving "not another's will" was
nowhere more keenly appreciated; and hard labor—or none at
all—and poor accommodations and plain fare were preferred as
long as independence was assured. [37] It was almost impossible, for
instance, for Mrs. Kirkland to hire a young girl to help her around
the house:

> "Well, I don't know," said Mrs. Ketchum in reply to my ques-
> tions; "there was a young lady here yesterday that was saying
> she didn't know but she'd live out a spell till she'd bought her
> a new dress."
> "Oh! but I wish to get a girl who will remain with me; I should
> not like to change often."
> Mrs. Ketchum smiled rather scornfully at this, and said there

were not many girls about here that cared to live out long at a
time.

My spirits fell at this view of the matter. Some of my dear
theorizing friends in the civilized world had dissuaded me most
earnestly from bringing a maid with me.

"She would always be discontented and anxious to return; and
you'll find plenty of good farmers' daughters ready to live with
you for the sake of earning a little money."

Good souls! how little did they know of Michigan! I have since
that day seen the interior of many a wretched dwelling, with almost literally nothing in it but a bed, a chest, and a table; children ragged to the last degree, and potatoes the only fare; but
never yet saw I one where the daughter was willing to own herself obliged to live out at service. She would "hire out" long
enough to buy some article of dress perhaps, or "because our
folks have been sick, and want a little money to pay the doctor,"
or for some such special reason; but never as a regular calling, or
with an acknowledgment of inferior station.[38]

This "republican spirit" was also obvious in the villagers' reluctance to admire anything which they themselves did not have.
Mrs. Kirkland recalled that her carpets were spoken of as "*one*
way to hide dirt"; her mahogany tables as "dreadful plaguy to
scour"; her kitchen conveniences as "lumberin' up the house for
nothin'."

One lady informed me, that if she had such a pantry full of
"dishes," under which general term is included every variety of
china, glass and earthenware, she should set up store, and "sell
them off pretty quick," for she would not "be plagued with
them." Another, giving a slighting glance at a French mirror of
rather unusual dimensions, larger by two thirds, I verily believe,
than she had ever seen, remarked, "that would be quite a nice
glass, if the frame was done over." [39]

As amusing, and irrational, as this aspect of "republican spirit"
was, the tenacity with which some Westerners held to their individualism was, for the Kirklands, an ugly spectacle when shiftless
men took advantage of their neighbors' generosity. Mrs. Kirkland
referred to Mr. B——, a "gentleman" who had squandered an in-
heritance and who then refused to work because pride and indo-
lence would not let him. What few comforts his family had were

given by charitable neighbors. "And these people, bringing with them such views and feelings . . . abuse Michigan," she wrote, "and visit upon their homely neighbors the bitter feelings which spring from . . . mortified and indomitable pride. Finding themselves growing poorer and poorer, they persuade themselves that all who thrive, do so by dishonest gains, or by mean sacrifices; and they are teaching their children, by the irresistible power of daily example, to despise plodding industry, and to indulge in repining and feverish longings after unearned enjoyments." [40]

Another family in the neighborhood was the Newlands, a squatter family who "sponged off" the Kirklands and their friends. The eldest daughter Amelia hired herself out long enough to buy a dress or to satisfy some other whim. When Mrs. Kirkland made a neighborly call at Christmastime, the Newlands were getting ready for a holiday party; she was surprised to see the cabin gaily trimmed and the table covered with food which neighbors had contributed. Amelia, a young woman with a shady reputation, was about to entertain her friends at a "kind of house-warmin'-like," Mrs. Kirkland was told. A few months later Amelia Newland was dead, apparently the victim of a murderous beating which one of her male companions had given her. "The class of settlers to which the Newlands belong, a class . . . too numerous in Michigan, is a vicious and degraded one," declared Mrs. Kirkland. "[They] have since left . . . the country, driving off with their own, [and] as many of their neighbors' cattle and hogs as they could persuade to accompany them." [41] The "unbridled license" of such people as the Newlands—the "off-casts," Crèvecoeur had called them—made equalitarianism in the Western wilderness a hypocrisy; and it was these excesses of the democratic spirit Mrs. Kirkland was sharply critical of in *A New Home*. "I cannot say that I feel much respect for any thing which looks like a willingness to live at others' cost," she asserted. [42]

Neighbors who held "such views and feelings" acted as though the world—Montacute, at least—owed them a living. [43] Their attitude—attributable in part, Mrs. Kirkland implied, to Andrew Jackson's special brand of democracy—was an application of the leveling spirit to the extreme: "one cannot help observing," she remarked tartly, "that 'levelling upwards' is much more congenial to 'human natur',' than levelling downwards. The man who thinks you ought to spare him a piece of ground for a garden, because

you have more than he thinks you need, would be far from sharing with his poorer neighbor the superior advantages of his lot.
He would tell him to work for them as *he* had done."

> Equality, perfect and practical, is the *sine qua non;* and any ap-
> pearance of a desire to avoid this rather trying fraternization, is
> invariably met by a fierce and indignant resistance. The spirit in
> which was conceived the motto of the French revolution, "La
> fraternité ou la mort," exists in full force among us, though modi-
> fied as to results. In cities we bestow charity—in the country we
> can only exchange kind offices, nominally at least. If you are per-
> fectly well aware that your nearest neighbor has not tasted meat
> in a month, nor found in his pocket the semblance of a shilling
> to purchase it, you must not be surprised, when you have sent
> him a piece, to receive for reply,
> "Oh! your pa wants to *change*, does he? Well, you may put it
> down." And this without the remotest idea that the time for re-
> payment ever will arrive, but merely to avoid saying, "I thank
> you," a phrase especially eschewed, so far as I have had oppor-
> tunity to observe.[44]

The Golden Rule in the West was largely giving on the part of the
"have's" and taking on the part of the "have not's." She was as
sharply critical of this concept of equality as Hugh Henry Brack-
enridge had been in *Modern Chivalry* (1815), and as Cooper was
in numerous books of social criticism; and she often took their
course in expressing disapproval: satire. Public opinion and atti-
tudes of mind—"the bugbear of the western country"—were too
strongly established; the idea of "let-a-be for let-a-be" did not
apply. "Whoever exhibits any desire for privacy is set down as
'praoud,' or something worse; no matter how inoffensive, or even
how benevolent he may be; and of all places in the world in which
to live on the shady side of public opinion, an American backwoods settlement is the very worst." [45] She talked a great deal
about her neighbors' pride, and she indulged Cooper's sentiment
about his fellow Americans: that Westerners had "the sensitive-
ness of [all] provincials," that they became "enraged when their
real faults [were] censured," that they were indeed *"raw-
[skinned]."* The comments hit her neighbors in a vulnerable spot.

It mattered little at the time to her Western neighbors that they
too might regard her provincial when she put on airs and graces,

that they too might call her *"raw-skinned."* She was to suffer from
hurt pride when she was the target of snide remarks from her
neighbors after her husband's mismanagement of land acquisi-
tions and land agents became common gossip. Ultimately, Mrs.
Kirkland learned one lesson the West had to teach: one didn't
poke fun at one's neighbors, not when one was a newcomer in their
midst. There was obvious truth in what she reported; but it was—
she herself said—an "unvarnished" truth that could rankle.

The Kirklands' awareness to the pressure of backwoods opinion,
their unpopular position in the village, indeed their hurt pride—
all these played a part in their decision to leave Michigan. Mrs.
Kirkland's intimate sketches did not make her popular with the
neighbors.[46] But their disenchantment with Western life was
deeper than just being caught on the "shady side of public
opinion." Scholarly, cultured people, they found the Western
wilderness not at all conducive to their inquiring minds and
not the place to make a home for their children. Everywhere
they saw that the struggle for survival in the wilderness created
an intense spirit of practicality; but there was more to living for
them than wrangling with land agents, listening to the gossip of
the women of the Montacute Female Beneficent Society, becoming
involved with petty lawsuits, or appeasing disgruntled democrats.
William Kirkland undoubtedly expressed their discontent in his
essay on the Western "paradise." Material or practical success,
their neighbors would agree, led inevitably on the Michigan
frontier to a feeling of equality—and mental or cultural accomplishments counted for nothing.

The real lack of Western living, the Kirklands discovered, was
that there was no concern for the "inner man"; the "outer man"
only dictated life in the clearings. For them at least, Mrs. Kirkland's words in *Forest Life* echoed a sad reality: the West was a
"scarce reclaimed wilderness" in which little advancement had
been made in "preparing the way for civilization, for intelligence,
for refinement, for religion. . . ." [47] Westerners were more interested, for the present at least, in living than in contemplating life.

However, if the Kirklands did not wholeheartedly endorse the
American dream as it was practiced in the West and if they did not
proclaim the perfectibility of Western man, they likewise did not
underestimate the promise of the West for many of their neighbors. That they appreciated the West is not denied and that they

cherished the freedom which the West gave is obvious from reading Kirkland's essay and *A New Home*. Although there were discomforts, there was a compensating pleasure in the primitive life:
Mrs. Kirkland ascribed much of the contentment men had to the
"heritage of the rural life," to the at-homeness they found in the
wilderness. Nevertheless, there was for them an insurmountable
barrier. "If people who have been born and bred in the country
find it difficult to form an idea of the splendor and importance of
the great [cities]," wrote Mrs. Kirkland the year before she and
her husband left Michigan, "those who have lived nowhere but in
that vortex of excitement can as little appreciate the calm, con-
templative quiet of a country life."

> The contrast can be imagined only by those who have tried
> both . . . the difference may be compared to that which marks
> the course of the Niagara;—in one place rapids and cataracts
> agitating the mighty flood till the air is filled with a brilliant spray,
> and [the] earth trembles to the deep-voiced roar of waters; and
> again, after only a single bend in the river, a glassy, waveless ex-
> panse, whose onward movement is scarcely perceptible. Over the
> one may now and then be discerned a glorious rainbow, but the
> other reflects always the green and peaceful shores, and the bright
> and steady lamps of heaven. Yet I suppose one must be like the
> fish, cold-blooded, to prefer the still water.[48]

Material success and physical contentment were not enough for
the appetite of the inner man who craved—indeed, required—
mental stimulus in order not to starve. The atmosphere Caroline
and William Kirkland breathed demanded the interaction of
thinking minds, the "mighty flood" of ideas, a number of keen
friends and acquaintances which for them only the East supplied.
The West was a paradise to many Americans in the 1830's and
1840's, but to them it proved to be a somewhat impoverished
Eden.

IV *Reception by the Critics*

A New Home was an eagerly read book. Americans—the great
majority, at least—did not know the West from firsthand experience; what they did know they had heard by word of mouth or
read in books. Visitors to the West saw the vast territory much as
the fiction writers had, and they passed the romantic visions on to

those who would listen. Mrs. Kirkland, therefore, had an immense advantage in writing what curious readers and reviewers could accept as the observations of "an actual settler."

Contemporary notices of *A New Home* in American and English journals suggested the real delight reviewers found in reading the book. Griswold, writing a few years later in *The Prose Writers of America,* summarized the critics' feeling when he recalled that no work of its kind was "more brilliantly successful than these original and admirable pictures of [the] frontier . . . [with their] genial humour, graphic description, and shrewd sense." The sketches had "strength, freshness, effect . . . simplicity [and] vigour." [49]

The reviewer in the New York *Mirror* hailed the book as a significant one in the young literature of the country. It was not simply another romance—"unwholesome food" which fiction-mongers too often whipped up to glut the public taste; it was a story about America—a "fire-side histor[y] which afford[ed] both instruction and amusement." Complaining about the novelists who filled their pages with "the usual trimmings" of romance, he welcomed "Mrs. Clavers" as a writer who "produce[d] from the materials of real life" a series of sketches about this "homespun life of ours." At last there was "some reality to [American] fiction." He was particularly pleased with the character sketches "all drawn to life, and made strikingly effective" and with the entertaining accounts of local manners. The review was a long one, longer than was usually found in the *Mirror;* and, unlike many reviews in the journals of the day, it was not padded with excerpts from the book itself to give its "flavour." It was obviously a happy assignment for the reviewer to write about *A New Home:* he knew of "no production superior to [it]" in commending the book to his readers. [50]

The critic in the *North American Review* thought that *A New Home* would bring Mrs. Kirkland an enviable reputation, "a work of striking merit; such as we do not often meet with in these days of repetition and imitation." The book was valuable for its fidelity to American life in the West because it spread no "romantic coloring" over the scenes described: "she has no paradise to offer him 'who'll follow'. . . . The real enjoyments of forest life are set forth in their true colors; but the real inconveniences and annoyances, and sacrifices, which belong to it, are not extenuated." And, after many pages of excerpts, he concluded that *A New Home* was "one of the most spirited and original works which have yet been produced in this country." [51]

The critic in the *Knickerbocker Magazine* especially liked the author's sprightly wit and spirit of fun: "with a keen eye for the ridiculous, and a ready appreciation of the burlesque; and with a remarkable knowledge of character, it is not . . . surprising that [she] should have written an amusing volume." She had done "good service" to her countrymen in giving them a completely honest account of life in the wilderness, not disguising the fact that comforts of life are hard to come by on the frontier—"that a moderate portion of its luxuries is rather a thing to be hoped for, than expected." And she had warned them against romantic misconceptions of the West, especially the "extravagant stories" speculators told to induce unsuspecting newcomers to buy land in the settlements.[52]

The journalist writing in the London *Literary Gazette* believed that the book gave a "more minute and faithful account of [the backwoodsmen's] daily life than any book of travels that has been published." [53] And the reviewer in the London *Athenaeum* recommended the book to those who had "appetite for what is humourous and graphic" in their reading. "The sketches were lively, fresh-coloured, and characteristic." Remembering the accounts of American life written by his own countrymen who had been in the United States, he declared that Mrs. Kirkland's "unflattering picture" of the backwoodsmen was more accurate, and sympathetic, than the "caricatures" sometimes drawn by English travelers: the portrait drawn by "that 'old woman'" Mrs. Frances Trollope, for instance, was "unnatural and repulsive, [while] Mrs. Clavers' sketches [were] natural and agreeable." [54]

Poe was perhaps the most appreciative and enthusiastic of Mrs. Kirkland's critics. *A New Home* created "an undoubted sensation," not so much because of its description and humor and character portrayal but because of its "*truth* and novelty." He saw in the sketches "a fidelity and vigor that prove[d] her pictures to be taken from the very life . . . 'scenes' that could have occurred only *as* and *where* she described them." He admitted that the portraits were so lifelike that she might well be charged with drawing specific individuals in parody; but she handled them dexterously, with freshness and freedom and, at times, with deep poignancy.

"Unquestionably," wrote Poe, "she is one of our best writers, has a province of her own, and in that province has few equals." [55]

Mrs. Kirkland doubtless had no equals in her day in her particular area of writing. The only work to approximate *A New Home* was William Byrd's *History of the Dividing Line* (1841), a book still little read in America (Irving would only hear of it in 1859)— the Virginia gentleman's satiric account of life in the North Carolina wilderness. Mrs. Kirkland herself said that she found the germ of her book in Mary Russell Mitford's "charming sketches" of English rural life; and, consciously or not, she probably owed a debt to Jane Austen's remarkable insight for character portrayal and masterful use of understatement. In *Forest Life* she also professed pleasure from reading "Major Jack Downing's" descriptions of Down-East characters, people who shared some of the foibles of her Western men and women.

But the warp and woof of her story was a fabric pretty much of her own making. She produced a memorable book with delightful character studies and with careful descriptions of scenes and places which the reader could largely appreciate. She wrote with honesty, candor, conviction, and a sprightly sense of humor. Although the style was feminine in its refinement and sophisticated in its tone, the book was written in a plain style breathing something of the Western air—pure, unrestrained, clear. Poe was right in praising the book as highly as he did. *A New Home,* a pioneer work in American realism, justified the opinion of Mrs. Kirkland's contemporaries. As Griswold said, the book might well become a "guide to those who . . . [were] labouring to create an American literature." [56]

CHAPTER 3

Forest Life and Western Clearings

My former sketches were of the safety-valve and flood-gate kind. They were the overflowings of a reservoir of new sights, new sounds, and new notions. They wrote themselves, so to speak. They were "First Impressions"—which . . . is the most fortunate title ever yet devised for a book of travels. First impressions are the only ones worth recording for the amusement or enlightenment of those who stay at home; and they must be arrested on the instant, or they lose their sparkle. It is in vain, after new things have become familiar, to attempt to make them amusing. The bead is gone forever.

—*Forest Life*

*F*orest Life and *Western Clearings* may not hold the reader's attention as *A New Home* did, precisely for the reason Mrs. Kirkland gives: they were not the result of "new sights, new sounds, and new notions." However, they may contain a different kind of interest; for, in the early chapters of *Forest Life,* it is apparent that she plans a new technique for this second book of Western impressions—what becomes in time the regionalist's technique. *Forest Life,* Mrs. Kirkland announced, was an "attempt to delineate some of the very ordinary scenes, manners and customs of Western life." "No wild adventures,—no blood-curdling hazards,—no romantic incidents,—" she continued, "occur within my limited and sober sphere." [1] "Amusement" was not so important as "enlightenment." She conceded that *Forest Life* was not so lively a book as *A New Home,* but she promised the reader that it was written with the assurance of one who was now "familiar" with Western peculiarities. "Common-place all," she maintained, "yet I must tell it." [2]

I *The Critics' Views*

Although the new technique confused most of the critics, who expected merely a sequel to *A New Home*, it was recognized by the astute reviewer in *Knickerbocker's*. He pointed out that *A New Home* had been a personal account of Western life—the West seen from the author's own perspective; it had been an amusing volume because it reflected Mrs. Kirkland's prejudices and convictions. In his opinion *Forest Life* was a more honest account of Western life because it was not so subjective; the book had a "warmer and more human tinge." Its "true attraction" lay in her discussions of "aspect[s] of society itself" and in her "graphic descriptions of nature and character." Perhaps his enthusiasm for the book was due to the fact that Mrs. Kirkland was now a fellow contributor to *Knickerbocker's;* but he was reminded as he read *Forest Life* of a certain regional quality he had previously noted in Catharine Maria Sedgwick's New England tales—a quality that captured for the reader characteristics of Massachusetts life years ago. "Miss Sedgwick must not only acknowledge a rival *near* her throne," he proclaimed, "but she must make room for a sister *on* it." The pictures of forest life, "interspersed as before with one or two admirable love-passages [the sentimental tales]," he declared, had an "interest vividly excited and [a] curiosity adroitly stimulated." And having exhausted his vocabulary of admiring phrases, he concluded simply: "these episodes, if we may so call them, are delightful." [3]

The majority of reviewers, however, were apparently not so aware as the *Knickerbocker* critic, and they said little in their columns—they were reluctant to write bad reviews but incapable of writing discerning ones. Indeed, Mrs. Kirkland rarely received during her literary career a bad notice from the professional reviewers, perhaps for any number of reasons: because of the soundness of her observations about the West; because of the moral tone of so much of the material, when morality in fiction was standard for the day; the fact that she was a woman; or the fact that she was a contributor and, in a very few years, a fellow reviewer. This reluctance to censure on the part of the reviewers, or simply an unawareness of Mrs. Kirkland's larger purpose, was apparent in the notice (reproduced in its entirety) which appeared in the *Democratic Review:*

No less graphic, witty, kindly, sensitive, and amusing a book than the predecessor of which it is a sequel. And agreeable as are both the volumes from beginning to end, there is no portion of either which we read with greater pleasure than the concluding intimation, that it is only "for the present" that the charming author, who still denies her real name to fame, takes her leave of the public. Her voice comes to us out of the far unknown wilderness from which she sends it forth, like the clear ringing song of a bird, issuing from the heart of the wood; although we may not see the sweet vocalist, nor distinguish the particular tree within whose shade it is hiding and singing, yet we listen with delight, and wait impatiently at every pause for another strain of the merry music.[4]

The writer, carried away by his own forest metaphor, expressed himself only in indifferent terms.

Indifference was surprising in Poe, who wrote a brief notice of *Forest Life*, the "very popular work" now in another reprinting, in 1845. Mrs. Kirkland was a close friend, even a contributor to the *Broadway Journal:*

As a narrative writer [Mrs. Clavers] deserves a place at the head of American female authors, and as a delineator of character she is greatly in advance of them all. Since her return to city life she has published nothing but an occasional sketch in a magazine; but the materials for a book are as abundant in our highways, as in the by-ways of the west. And we hope to see an announcement before long, of a work from her hand, sketching the peculiarities of city life, wherein she would be free to exercise her fine powers of observation, with not the fear of displeasing one of their high mightinesses, the editors of pictorial magazines. It is not a little remarkable that these gentlemen are extremely fond of tales of love, seeing that they generally have so little of that commodity themselves, except for themselves.[5]

Avoiding specific comment about the book, Poe parried it with the alternative that she write city sketches (an alternative, incidentally, that Mrs. Kirkland may have followed a few years later when she did write such sketches for the *Union* and probably for *Putnam's*). Poe obviously was a perceptive critic in many instances, as his comment about *A New Home* demonstrated; and his apparent ignorance of Mrs. Kirkland's larger purpose in *Forest*

Life may perhaps be explained by his own harried life at the time. Probably he, like many reviewers, had not read the book; but he wanted to say something kind about his friend.

Nonetheless, reviewers had—for whatever the reason—polite reservations. *Forest Life* "is, on the whole, less interesting than [*A New Home*]," wrote the critic in the *North American;* "not from any failure in the author's powers, but because it does not come upon us with the gloss of novelty that gave such charm to the other." He admitted that Mrs. Kirkland had once again caught the color of Western life in the sketches appearing in the second book, far better—in his opinion—than had Seba Smith and Thomas C. Haliburton in their Down-East sketches; still, *Forest Life* "is but a continuation of the original plan." [6] Repetition, he implied, without larger vision served no purpose.

Sameness and feminine affectation bothered the reviewer in *Graham's;* to him, *Forest Life* would be "charming volumes, written with a freshness and spirit that delights and would surprise us were we not familiar with the first work of their author." He did not wish to appear "difficult and ungracious," but there was for him "too frequent [an] introduction of French words and phrases —not, certainly, from vanity, for no woman has less affectation than our author—but doubtless from habit and a desire of condensation. A pithy French phrase of three words, *to those who understand the language,* will frequently convey more meaning than half a dozen English lines; but Mrs. Clavers," he admonished, "there are in this world a vast number of very decent people who know as little French as a politician does honesty." [7]

When *Western Clearings,* a miscellany with half the material having been previously published in magazines, appeared four years later, the reviewers were only mildly interested in the book. They praised the author not so much for the recent collection but for what she had already accomplished in her sketches of Western life. Admittedly, *Western Clearings* is not the intimate narrative *A New Home* was; it is not the insightful history *Forest Life* was; it is a bitter view of frontier life. Yet the critics once again were considerate.

The book, said the writer in the London *Spectator,* wanted "the freshness which distinguished her *New Home.*" And inviting readers to make the comparison, he set the apologetic tone for his review: "In spite, however, of tales whose structure rather reminds one of Annual literature, and of a style which has but slight congruity with the subject matter, *Western Clearings* [hardly] sustains the interest of the reader. . . . We see . . . that [although] the substance has been drawn from life, [and] the artist . . . [has] arranged and heightened matters for effect . . . the present volume is inferior to *A New Home.*" [8]

Another critic, beginning his comments with a reference to *A New Home*—that "lively, descriptive volume on the *far-west*"— called *Western Clearings* simply "another gathering from the same fold." Of course, the writer deferred, almost any account of life "as it exists in the back states" should be "worth listening to"— particularly when it was presented by an author whose "literary dexterity, and an unusually keen mind for the ludicrous" had brought her considerable attention.[9] The reporter for the Boston *Courier,* writing a pre-publication notice, spoke not of *Western Clearings* but of Mrs. Kirkland's earlier work: "She writes of what she [has] seen, and her descriptions are fresh, vivid, and natural . . . her vein of humor [is] original, and she has a happy power of seizing and delineating peculiarities of human character. Her descriptions of Western life and manners have been received with great favor, on both sides of the Atlantic, from their truth and freshness. They are contributions to American literature." [10] But, like his fellow reviewers, he did not write excitedly about the book.

Nor did her friends Bryant and Poe show much enthusiasm for the book. Bryant stressed the "reputation" she had already acquired, "which gives all she writes a quick circulation over the whole country." Avoiding specific reference to *Western Clearings,* he continued: "Some of the Great Westerners . . . have been offended by the freedom of her satire. . . . Yet as sprightly as her tales appear, they have running through the whole of them an undercurrent of profounder meaning.— Her sympathies are genial," Bryant iterated; "while detecting the faults, she does full justice to the nobler qualities of the Western settlers." [11] When Poe wrote a notice for the *Broadway Journal,* his comment, like Bryant's, was primarily an estimate of the author, her character, and her previous work; and it was incorporated later with little change in "The Literati of New York City." *Western Clearings* was, Poe briefly summarized, "a collection of graphic Tales, each illustrative of the customs, manners and ideas of a peculiar people, and descriptive of a new and uncivilized, but great and growing country." [12]

II *Mrs. Kirkland's View*

Of the critics, perhaps only Bryant and Poe discovered in time why their friend chose to write what seemed to be two rather dull books—why she deliberately changed her technique in these books. Admittedly, she did not want to antagonize her Western neighbors; for the deft touches of the artist's brush so often used in limning individuals—herself included—in *A New Home* were in the later volumes discarded for broader strokes which made less personal the character portraits. "I shall not consider myself," she asserted in the preface to *Forest Life,* "a foreign tourist, whose one stinging truth, though varnished over with a thick layer of compliment, shall rankle in the sensitive heart of my [Western] countrymen long after the flattery is forgotten." And, at the end of the book, she again announced her intent:

> When I began this second attempt to note some of the peculiarities of the Western settler's life, it was my intention to . . . [dwell] rather more upon such portions of our experience as related principally to our own simple selves. But before I had proceeded far I made the discovery that the day had gone by for such plain personal reminiscences as filled the pages of "A New Home." A stranger, feeling as a stranger, equally indifferent to all, writes with a freedom which a friend and neighbor of several years' standing must renounce entirely. It is impossible to describe minutely our own personal experience without giving in some degree the experience of others; and this is a matter requiring careful handling, to say the least. We may say of ourselves what we must not say of others. We may describe our own log-house, but woe betied us if we should make it appear that any body else lived in one! We may tell of our own blunders, but we must beware how we touch upon the blunders of others.[13]

Her object—she wanted to make it very clear—was to "[venture] only upon a general outline of truth, with a saving veil of acknowledged fiction." [14] If thrusts of the satirist's pen had caused ill-feeling in *A New Home,* they would not be repeated. Satire was the tool of the writer who felt himself superior to his material, as Mrs. Kirkland had felt when she wrote her first book. It was no longer effective when one's attitude changed, as it had when she began to write *Forest Life*. She would now write with some authority about a way of life unfamiliar to the reader, indeed unfamiliar to Mrs. Kirkland herself a few years before. "Who [is] more justly entitled to the privilege of speaking the truth about us than one of our very selves," she asked, "—one whose lot is cast in, for better for worse, with the settlers of the backwoods." "I eschew and disclaim all notice of the older settlements—the towns and villages in which the spirit of emulation and of imitation has nearly annihilated all that was characteristic of new country life. Of these I have nothing to say; for has not their aspect been painted a thousand times? There is still a dash of Western wildness about them, it is true;—a freshness of coloring may still be traced by a close observer;—but my theme lies elsewhere, and this should be borne in mind." [15]

The larger vision in *Forest Life* points forward to the concern of the regionalist who, writing his stories and sketches in the years following the Civil War, looked for the provincial characteristics in the scenes he described. Regarded in this light, *Forest Life* is a milestone in American literary experience. Not only had Mrs. Kirkland brought realism to the pages of *A New Home*, but now she introduced regionalism to some of the material in *Forest Life* —anticipating by a generation what her son and other writers would be addressing themselves to in their fiction.

III   *Forest Life*

Forest Life was so indefinite in form as to defy classification— sentimental tales, sketches, poetry, anecdotes, abbreviated travel narratives, and autobiography. Of immediate appeal to Mrs. Kirkland's women readers, and some critics, were the sentimental tales which ran through many chapters. Three of them occupied a third of the book, identifying through the characters' actions the virtues and vices of mid-century conduct and example. The "good" always triumphed, the "bad" saw the error of their ways—as was the case with Caroline Hay, the young Western lass loved by a simple country lad. Caroline, having lived for a time in the city with relatives, returned home with airs and graces. The country lad, as in so many sentimental tales, performed a feat of courage which won Caroline's reluctant heart and her benefactor's indebtedness. Offered a well-paying position in the city, Seymour declined it for Caroline and life in the woods:

> A wedded life begun by an act of virtuous sacrifice [Mrs. Kirkland reminded the reader] can scarcely fail to be a happy one. That complacency of temper which sheds light over the darkest hour is never more surely nourished than by the habitual pleasure of doing good and conferring happiness. Seymour is Mr. Hay's right hand, and his influence and that of his fair and gracious Caroline is a daily blessing to the younger members of both families. I feel assured that we shall be able to point to them half a dozen years hence as a proof that cultivation and refinement are any thing but lost in the country.[16]

Another of these tales introduced one of Mrs. Kirkland's most memorable Western characters—Aunty Parshalls, a wizened little woman with an intense love for her erring family. Nearly half the second volume was devoted to an account of the Sibthorpes, an English couple who had settled in the American West. She copied their "letters" (eleven in all, written to friends in England) in which they expressed their respect for life and manners in the West.

Of more immediate appeal to the modern reader is the regional material. Bearing in mind her larger purpose, Mrs. Kirkland informs the reader: "My rambles will . . . carry me all over our beautiful state." If on occasion she speaks of localized towns or villages, she "mean[s] the history of one settlement to include that of many. . . ."[17] And still showing a shadow of resentment at the old accusations leveled by her neighbors, she adds:

> . . . I take this opportunity to declare that all the naughty and unpleasant people—all the tattlers and mischief-makers,—all the litigious,—all the quarrelsome,—all the expectorant,—all the unneat,—all the unhandsome,—have emigrated to Iowa, Wiskonsan, or Texas, or some other far distant land . . . and that there is not—*meo periculo*—one single specimen of any of these classes remaining in this wide peninsula. So that any description of such characters which I may hazard in future must be mere phantoms of the brain, and cannot have been drawn from real life within these bounds. Some subjects being thus precluded, I shall content myself with offering . . . general sketches of life and its chances and changes. . . .[18]

Her rambles take her on a wagon tour of the Michigan hinterland where she looks for "general" Western curiosities: the ague,
hospitality, the beauties of nature, the Westerners' fondness for
pork, public education. She writes about common experiences fac-
ing the Michigan pioneer: raising a mill, summer flies and mos-
quitoes, funerals, electioneering, hardships, "good neighbors," a
donation party for a clergyman. Although she may have been
amused by the small talk of the ladies of the Montacute Female
Beneficent Society, she has discovered her neighbors' delight in
chit-chat: "I . . . [confess] that my foible (if I have one) is love
of gossip. I am no great tea-drinker, nor yet an immoderate
snuffer; I am not able to knit a stocking during a ride of ten miles
on a hard-trotting horse; nor have I taken geese away from home
to pick rather than refuse an invitation for an afternoon visit. . . .
There are people that excel me in the true tokens of gossiping—
yet I am a hopeful scholar . . . a candidate for secondary honors
at least." [19]

Humor once again is Mrs. Kirkland's ready ally, but now she
sees herself and her Western friends from a new vantage point:

> At first nothing is more natural than to think and speak of the
> contrasts that are shocking us at every turn, but a few years'
> familiarity with what we dislike makes it nearly indifferent. As far
> as modes of speech are concerned, we find ourselves much more
> likely to adopt unconsciously the quaint and incorrect expressions
> that assail our ears in daily intercourse, than to inspire our neigh-
> bors with a desire for habits of greater correctness; and after this
> assimilation takes place, we do not recollect to describe what at
> first seemed so odd. I confess myself to have become too much
> Westernized to be a competent painter of Western peculiarities. [20]

"One sees the rougher sort of people in their best light," she ad-
mits elsewhere in the book, "and learns to own the 'tie of brotherhood.'" [21]

On the wagon tour, she and her husband met a family from the
East newly arrived in Michigan, and she took a Westerner's delight in pointing out their "peculiarities." The Margolds, in fact,
were rather close portraits of the Kirklands when they first arrived
on the frontier. The Margolds complained about the accommodations when they stopped for a night with a poor Western family—
more clamorously but in much the same spirit as the Kirklands

had when they had stopped at the Ketchums in *A New Home*.
Although the farmer and his wife offered what they had of comfort and food, the Margolds, insensitive to the hospitality, thought
only of their own discomfort. On leaving, the husband tried to
pay a sum of money to the poor man. "*You* didn't think [we] was
*on*civil, did ye?" the injured farmer retorted.

In the wagon en route to the next settlement, Mrs. Margold,
making plain her annoyance, earned a Western reproof from the
teamster whom her husband had hired:

> "I never did see such an odious country as this!" she exclaimed;
> "it is impossible to look decent for an hour!"
> "Well! one comfort is," said Mr. Butts consolingly, "that there
> a'n't many folks to see how bad you look, here in the woods! We
> a'n't used to seein' folks look dreadful slick nother—so it don't
> matter." [22]

And returning the banknote Mr. Margold had left at the farm-
house, the teamster made another point: "You see, he a'n't no
hand to make a fuss . . . so he jist told me to give it to ye after
you got away. And he said . . . he'd rather you'd buy manners
with it, if you could." [23] Humor in *Forest Life* was directed not
toward the Westerner but against the newly arrived emigrant in
the West. Mrs. Kirkland, now aware of her neighbors' feelings,
had found instruction in behavior which was once her own.

IV *Regional Material*

When one gets beyond transient interests in the book, he recog-
nizes the regional material which most profoundly marks the pages
of *Forest Life*. The character of Western life ultimately infuses
the book—a life that is rugged, often shabby, frequently exacer-
bating. And that character is traced in a fanciful incident Mrs.
Kirkland relates at the beginning of the narrative.

On setting out on the wagon tour, she borrowed from "a political friend" a very special pair of eyeglasses he had once used during a campaign—"magic glasses" which would enable her in the
tour of observation "to give the most fascinating and satisfactory
accounts of all I saw and heard." Supplied with "two or three
capacious note-books" in which to jot down impressions along the
way and wearing the newly acquired "optics," she looked about

her, ready to pen the first thought that flew into her mind. "We were passing over Smoke Hill," she wrote, "—an elevation which had always before appeared to me covered with stunted oak bushes, relieved at intervals by a huge stump or a girdled tree. What was my surprise to find its gently-swelling sides planted with luxurious sugar-maples and lofty elms, with fantastic arbors formed here and there amid their stately trunks by garlands of honey-suckle and eglantine." The tour already seemed to afford such a "rare splendor" of delights to the senses. "Cottages . . . [were] roofed with golden thatch, and enriched with mosses . . . and every door [was] surrounded with its group of lovely mothers, and children . . . and . . . gushing streams of crystal water sparkled and whispered along beds of silver sand." Even the old lumber wagon she and her husband were traveling in, she observed for the first time, was "fresh painted and resplendently varnished . . . while old Dobbin and Dagon had . . . coats well brushed, and harness which gave back . . . the rays of the burning sun."

When her husband stopped at a cottage to ask for water, "one of those charming mothers" whom she had been passing along the way addressed her:

"Lovely lady!" she began, ". . . will you let my Coralie look for one moment at your glasses?"

Who could hesitate? In an instant the precious loan of my friend was intrusted to the dimpled fingers of an infant cherub; in another,—lay scattered in a million of fragments on the ground!

"Well! I swan!" exclaimed the mamma, giving a round box on the ear to a dirty little urchin; "what made you let the little hussy have your specs?"

I raised my aching eyes to her face, and stood speechless. Why should I describe the dingy locks,—the check-apron,—the shoeless feet of the [child]. . . . Why picture anew a tumble-down log-house, with its appropriate perfumes of milk-emptins, bread, and fried onions? Why speak of Dobbin and Dagon, shorn of their beams, and lopping down their heads, to crop the scrub-oaks . . . or of the old wagon, patched and mended . . . ?

The "magic glasses" were shattered; the faery spell was broken. "It is needless to dwell on these particulars," she concluded. "It is painful to tell of log-causeways, now seeming rougher than of old,

or of rustic maidens, looking coarse . . . [in] contrast with the
[recent] illusions. . . . Homeward I took my melancholy way,
resolutely closing my eyes upon prospects of merely ordinary
beauty, which I knew would be . . . divested even of their real
charms, and concluding in my own mind it would be better to
content myself with seeing with my own eyes." [24] Her own eyes—
cleared now of the chimerical vision of the magic spectacles—recorded for the inquisitive reader the "homely and primitive aspect
of our vicinity." [25]

What truly identified the character of Western life was what it
did to individuals. If people arrived in the fabled West, "a land
flowing with milk and honey," full of hope and aspiration, they
became in the passage of time disillusioned and exhausted.
Strength, physical and moral, was enervated: environment sapped
the initiative, and people burdened by the workaday routine grew
listless. Women became slovenly; men became lazy. Mrs. Ains-
worth, an emigrant from New York State, learned to "accommo-
dat[e]":

> She . . . cut from the butter-plate with her own knife, and
> dip[ped] her tea-spoon time and again into the dish of preserves
> intended for the whole company, without a misgiving. If a wash
> basin was required, she could not see where was the harm of
> using for that purpose the bowl, which would in a few minutes
> be on duty on the breakfast table, and she did not mind mislaying
> her pocket-handkerchief, since an apron did just as well for her.
> She always washed and combed in the kitchen, though she had
> a bedroom adjoining, and she . . . appropriate[d] the space
> under her bed to her husband's best boots, a spare bridle or two,
> and the saddle when it happened to be at home: it was "so
> handy." [26]

Women were the grumblers in Michigan, Mrs. Kirkland had
pointed out in *A New Home;* but they were so with reason:
"Many of them . . . made sacrifices for which they were not at
all prepared and which detract[ed] largely from their every day
stores of comfort." [27]

The women and their husbands plodded on day in and day out,
dulled by the arduous work, indifferent to change—"not mak[ing]
the slightest effort towards any thing beyond bare utility" and
toiling all their lives "for little more than a living." [28] They had be-

come so wearied by the daily routine they were unable to visualize that it might be better: "[they] look[ed] neither to the right hand nor to the left—notic[ed] nobody's plans but their own—eschew[ed] every thing like experiment—observ[ed] no necessity for improvement in implements or modes of tillage—[felt] too poor to take an agricultural paper, and too busy to read one —and so [went] on, from year to year, plodding circuitous paths." . . .[29]

A dull, aching anger assailed the men; and they became sullen like Mr. B—— or like the Newlands in *A New Home,* or shiftless like the farmer in *Forest Life* who sat about the house "in listless idleness."[30] Sometimes they resorted to liquor to deaden the ache, as Mr. Ketchum had in *A New Home,* or to the "imbecile despair" of keeping school, as Mr. Whicher had in *A New Home.*[31] Like the indolent farmers of North Carolina whom Byrd had spoken of in *History of the Dividing Line,* they let their wives do the farm work and became village idlers. The greatest exertion Aunty Parshalls' husband engaged in, Mrs. Kirkland reported, was "to walk over to the village in the morning, and sit smoking on the tavern steps or in the store all day; laying down the law on all disputed points for the instruction of the hordes of idlers who are always to be found about those places."[32]

Some idlers, proposing to escape the humdrum farm routine, tried other expediencies—such as running for elective offices in the county. Simeon Jenkins, whom Mrs. Kirkland had introduced in *A New Home,* explained his attitude: "I farm altogether by the book. I consider headwork to be by far the most important, so I generally let my boys perform the manual labor, while I exercise my mind in planning work for them. Farming requires a great deal of reflection, and I never could reflect much while I was hard at work."[33]

Yet even idleness might be preferred, Mrs. Kirkland implied, to another warping feature of Western life—envy. It was outrage at what seemed to be the perverse injustices of life that prompted the Newlands, when they had left Montacute, to take with them some of their neighbors' stock, thereby avenging themselves for their own sense of humiliation. It was not pleasant, Mrs. Kirkland remarked dryly, "to find a dead pig in one's well, or a favorite dog hung up at the gate-post; to say nothing of cows milked on the marshes, hen-roosts rifled, or melon-patches cleared in the course of the night." [34]

Fighting the wilderness was in itself an humiliating experience. Trees were a mortal enemy that the pioneer attacked savagely. He saw them only as "obstacles which must be removed, at whatever sacrifice," Mrs. Kirkland declared, "to make way for mills, stores, blacksmiths' shops,—perhaps churches,—certainly taverns. 'Clearing' is his daily thought and nightly dream; and so literally does he act upon this guiding idea, that not one tree, not so much as a bush, of natural growth, must be suffered to cumber the ground. . . . The very notion of advancement, of civilization, of prosperity, seems inseparably connected with the total extirpation of the forest." [35] The starkness of the Western landscape after the backwoodsman had cleared the land and burned the stumps for fields and homesites startled the unknowing observer. Trees were hastily logged or milled, and cabins or frame buildings were hurriedly erected with little care because there was always the more important farm work to do. In a little time log cabins were tumble-down in need of paint and general repair; public buildings like the schoolhouse in Montacute "gathered blackness . . . [and] had as yet no taste of paint." [36] Not a tree shielded the barrenness. "I wish our people cared more for the beautiful," Mrs. Kirkland lamented.[37]

But the Westerner did not see beauty in the trees, as Mrs. Kirkland well knew. The wilderness was rank, raw, relentless, indestructible. Saplings took root seemingly overnight in newly prepared fields; the public square in Montacute, cleared only a short while before for a park, was already thick with weeds, "the work of a passing flock of sheep, which sowed it thickly with Canada thistles . . . [that] have yielded a crop sufficient to supply all the country round." [38] Subduing, even controlling, the wilderness in town or country was a desperate battle; and men frequently grew bitter or restless because of the odds against them.

"Our neighbors," Mrs. Kirkland remarked, "seem bit with the strange madness of ceaseless transit, flitting mostly westward, like ghosts that shun the coming day." Many of them, living on their third or fourth farm, were hoping somehow to escape the sense of despair that plagued their lives and were seeking in their "blundering search after happiness" to find an eventual El Dorado.

And, after they had "buil[t] a log-house, fence[d] a dozen acres or so, plough[ed] half of them, girdle[d] the trees, and then [sold] out to a new comer, one whose less resolute spirit [had] perhaps quailed a little before the difficulties of the untouched forest," they pushed farther west.[39] The grass was greener farther on: forests gave way to broad prairies, life promised to be less arduous, the soil was equally fertile:

> . . . if we see now and then a great wagon with its [passengers] . . . we do not expect to see it make a final stop in our Main Street. We know that it is destined for the deep woods [and prairies] far beyond us . . . that the stout farmer . . . has tired of his Michigan farm, and is going out to the "diggings" in Illinois, Wiskonsan, or Iowa. He only stops long enough . . . to refresh his weary wife and children, and to buy provisions for a further march, and then bravely sets forth again, to eat and sleep in the woods as long as may be necessary. If you should ask him why he thus forsakes all that most of us think worth living for, he would tell you . . . that he thinks there is more room at the West; that a poor man can get along better where there is not so many folks; and that he can get twice as much good land . . . where the country is quite new. If you ask his wife how she likes the change, she will try perhaps to put the best face on the matter, and say that she hated to break up, but th' old man thought he could do better for the children;—or if she be of the more timid and gentle nature, (as there are indeed many in this rough West,) she will answer with silent tears, which however will be carefully concealed from her husband.[40]

And yet, Mrs. Kirkland intimated, their new lot would be no easier.

Wilderness life, she maintained, was characterized by conflicts and contrasts—often exasperating, sometimes amusing. If the land did not induce apathy, anger, or futile despair among the hardier Westerners, it certainly developed among plain and practical people a sense of expediency. The soil in Michigan was a rich sandy loam, which could become the veritable garden Hoffman had spoken about. Although Mrs. Kirkland urged her neighbors in *A New Home* to plant such "exotic" vegetables as asparagus, cauliflower, and pumpkins, they sowed only the useful vegetables and grain: "wheat and indian corn, and oats, and buckwheat turn directly into one's pocket." [41] " 'Taters grow in the fields, and 'taters is good enough for me," she was told.[42] Cauliflower and celery were "mere superfluities," tomatoes were "heathenish and abominable," "asparagus [was] useful only to put above the looking-glass as a fly-trap." [43] Even Mrs. Kirkland admitted that "we ought all to have good gardens by this time, but then we have so much else to do." [44]

Wilderness living prompted an urgency for the expedient. Women saved themselves for the necessary work around the farm or in the home. When Mrs. Kirkland protested that the sheets on the beds in a shabby tavern she stopped in were dirty, the chambermaid replied: "you see, ma'am, we've had sich lots of company . . . and so all of our sheets but these is a drying in the kitchen —not aired enough yet to put upon the beds,—and we thought you'd like these better, 'cause they're so much healthier! you know damp sheets is dreadful unwholesome—and there ha'n't nobody slept in these but some *very* nice gentlemen!" [45] The ladies at a quilting party Mrs. Kirkland attended were given a noon meal; afterward, the hostess "went all around to the different plates, selecting such pieces of cake as were but little *bitten,* and paring off the half demolished edges with a knife . . . replace[d] them in their original circular position in the dishes. When this was accomplished, she assiduously scraped from the edges of the plates the scraps of butter that had escaped demolition, and wiped them back on the remains of the pat." [46]

Women doctored family sicknesses because physicians were often many miles away, and their fees were often high. They became herb women who sought among the Western plants the one which was, for them, the most beneficial. Folk remedies and folk beliefs were equally compounded in their cures:

"That everlastin' [an herb woman told Mrs. Kirkland] is a prime thing to wrap up the axe in, after you've cut yourself a choppin'. As long as that keeps moist, the wound'll keep cool and easy. The bees knows the good of it, for when they've been a fightin', you'll always see 'em a huntin' for everlastin', if there is any, and they go and get it for to heal 'em up. But bees is dreadful knowin' critters! They understand what you say jist as well as any body. If there's any body dies in the house, they'll all go away if you don't take no notice on 'em; but if you go and talk to 'em, and tell 'em that sich a one is dead, (calling him by name,) and hang a black cloth over the hive, and tell the bees if they'll stay

you'll do well by 'em, why, they'll stay, and go to work peaceable.
. . . bees won't never thrive well unless you talk with 'em; you
must take your knittin' work and go and sit by 'em, and tell 'em
things, and talk about the neighbors and sich, or they'll get lonesome and discouraged, and your honey'll be all bee-bread. Now,
honey is one o' the best things you can have in your family, for
it's good sweetnin' for any thing—cake or coffee, or any thing.
You take a table-spoonful of coffee to five quarts of water, and
sweeten it well with honey, and bile it about an hour, and it'll be
as good coffee as any body need to wish to drink. To be sure it
gives some folks the corry-mobbley, but I know how to cure that,
jist as easy! Take and stew angle-worms, and spread a plaster on
'em, and lay it on your stomick, and drink red-pepper tea bilin'
hot, and see how quick the pain'll leave ye!" [47]

Expediency sometimes required a stoical unconcern on the part
of neighbors. Mrs. Kirkland told how her blood "nearly curdled"
when a neighbor—a farmer who had been crushed by a fallen
tree and could not live—was measured for a coffin before he had
died. When she protested to the carpenter, he replied simply and
practically: "Oh, he was past knowing any thing, poor fellow, and
they got his woman out of the room for a few minutes. You know,
ma'am, such things must be done, and the sooner the better." [48]
Expediency was evident too in the notorious habit of borrowing, which had so plagued the Kirklands in *A New Home*. Rather
than go home and "dress up" for the tea which Mrs. Kirkland was
about to serve some neighbors, Mrs. Nippers, the redoubtable gossip of Montacute, declared:

"If you could lend me a smart cap and cape, I don't know but I
would [stay]." So she was ushered in due form to my room, with
unbounded choice in a very narrow circle of caps and capes, and
a pair of thin shoes, and then clean stockings, were successively
added as decided improvements to her array. And when she made
her appearance in the state-apartments, she looked, as she said
herself, "pretty scrumptious"; but took an early opportunity to
whisper, "I didn't know where you kept your pocket-handker-
chiefs." So Alice was dispatched for one, and the lady was complete.[49]

Because life in the clearings, even for the hardier pioneers, was
"hopelessly humdrum," [50] they tried to escape the aching sense of
alienation from old friends back East; of isolation from neighbors

many miles away; of loneliness "which is apt to beset the heart or
the imagination . . . in moments of depression, or long hours of
ill health." [51] To combat these frustrations, Westerners in their
precious easeful moments searched for companionship at funerals,
which were always hugely attended; delighted in picnics and
quilting bees, donation parties and *charivaris;* traveled miles to
attend church or to help in house, barn, and mill raisings. New
arrivals to the West were greeted cordially, accepted openly, pro-
nounced "'nice people' . . . [whom] we think we shall like . . .
very well if they stay long enough for our present favorable impression to take root." [52] People *needed* to be neighborly, and even
those who had little of this world's goods shared what they had
with friends and strangers. "Hospitality," declared Mrs. Kirkland,
"is, I believe, *invariably* rendered among us, with a freedom
worthy of Arcadia itself."

> . . . I have never known or heard of an instance [she continued]
> where those who have found it convenient to throw themselves
> on the kindness of a settler of any degree, have not been received
> with a frank welcome, which has appeared to me peculiarly ad-
> mirable, because extended, in many cases, under circumstances of
> the greatest inconvenience. Nor have I ever known compensation
> demanded, whatever may have been the trouble given; and where
> it has been accepted at all, it has been only sufficient to repay
> actual cost, and that usually upon urgency.[53]

Fire—one of the gravest hazards of the wilderness—which swept
so easily through log cabins, or was fanned so swiftly through
fields, and death which often came tragically or gratuitously were
immediate signals for neighborly assistance. A term of highest respect afforded anyone in the West was that he was a good neighbor, a phrase "much more comprehensive than that which can be
found in the dictionary." [54]

Of course, good neighbors were as rare in the West as elsewhere. More often there were "nosey" neighbors who talked over
everyone's private affairs "without stint or measure" and whose
duty it became "to ferret them out." [55] Mr. Whicher, the village
schoolmaster for a term, "never saw a letter or a sealed paper of
any kind that he did not deliberately try every possible method,
by peeping, squeezing, and poking, to get at its content." [56] One of
Mrs. Kirkland's hired girls "made herself entirely at home, looking

into my trunks, &c., and asking the price of various parts of my dress." [57]

Although such nosiness might be exasperating, it was a way to relieve the tedium. "Next to talking about ourselves," Mrs. Kirkland admitted, "the pleasantest thing is talking about our neighbors." [58] She welcomed the company of the eccentric pipe-smoking Cleory Jenkins, the loquacious Mrs. Titmouse, even the queen of "fiddle-faddle" in Montacute, Mrs. Nippers—gossips all. Indeed, delight in gossip and a desire to break the monotony of wilderness life prompted Mrs. Kirkland herself to write two books and a number of articles for magazines.

Humor also played a significant part in relieving the monotony. *Charivaris* and house raisings were occasions for broad farce, which men particularly engaged in. It sometimes took good-natured cajoling to get a house raised in one day under the nervous eye of a "boss":

> " 'Ta'n't play-spell, boys!" said the "boss."
> "Law! I tho't 'twas! I seen the master out o' doors," replied one of the [boys].
> "Well, now you know it a'n't, you'd better keep your teeth warm," shouted the master in return; "put your tongue in your elbow, and then may-be you'll work!" [59]

And petty lawsuits occupied the attention of villagers and farmers —lawsuits usually unimportant and trifling but cases offering amusement to the people assembled in the court, perhaps even to the litigants themselves. Mrs. Kirkland spoke of a slander suit brought by a tailor in Montacute against one of the town's tongue-waggers. The women of the village sided with the accused: "Each wished to tell 'the truth, the whole truth, and nothing but the truth'; and to ask one question, elicited never less than one dozen answers; the said answers covering a much larger ground than the suit itself, and bringing forward the private affairs and opinions of half the village. In vain did [the judge] roar 'silence!' his injunctions only made the ladies angry, and of course gave their tongues a fresh impetus." The case was settled when the husband of the accused paid the tailor for damages—"three dollars and fifty cents worth of lumber for his character"—and the wife "unsa[id] all she had said." [60]

Bad fences, missing dogs, unruly cattle, pigs' ears, and women's tongues [Mrs. Kirkland wrote], are among the most prolific sources of litigation; to say nothing of the satisfactory amount of business which is created by the collection of debts. . . . These suits are so frequent, that they pass as part and parcel of the regular course of things.[61]

Even though such litigations were inconsequential, they were, Mrs. Kirkland confessed, "rather . . . enjoyed."[62]

Isolation encouraged a rugged independence, a resoluteness, a determination on the part of the Westerner to win the struggle against the wilderness—to prove one's mettle to oneself and one's neighbors. "If I were called on to state the quality which more than any other formed the especial characteristic of the Western settler," Mrs. Kirkland reported, "I should name Self-dependence —a direct manifestation of that which has been given as a national bias—Individualism."[63] It showed in the family where the father was usually given a deference he could not expect elsewhere: "He would as soon give up his right hand as relinquish this supremacy."[64] It was a supremacy earned by diligence and ingenuity. Farmers were "self-taught" in the ways of the wilderness, becoming jacks-of-all-trades: "the invention of new modes of supplying [daily] wants; the substitution of one thing for another; the application of the same article to many different purposes, all of which . . . [were] quite different from the one for which it was originally designed."[65] This individualism made the weak envious and the strong proud—pride in accomplishment through one's own efforts.

Individualism encouraged a feeling of self-importance among the Western settlers and led inevitably to that one trait so irksome to the Kirklands in *A New Home*—an unwillingness to put themselves in what was regarded an "inferior station."[66] The teamster who was hired by the family lately arrived in the West objected to unloading the luggage from the wagon: "look here, uncle! I want you to take notice of one thing—I didn't engage to wait upon ye. I a'n't nobody's nigger, mind that! I'll be up to my bargain. I came on for a teamster. If you took me for a servant, you're mistaken. . . ."[67] And, when the new family persisted in treating their hosts cavalierly, the husband angrily retorted:

My family were willing to accommodate you as far as they could; such as we had, you were welcome to, but we are poor, and have not much to do with. Now, you haven't seemed to be satisfied with any thing, and your behavior has hurt my wife's feelings, and mine too. You think we are poor ignorant people, and so we are; but you think we haven't feelings like other folks, and there you are mistaken. . . . it's my desire that you pick up your things and drive on to the next tavern, where you can call for what you like, and pay for what you get. I don't keep a tavern, though I'm always willin' to entertain a civil traveller as well as I can.[68]

Travelers to the West discovered, as the Kirklands had, that "there are places where the 'almighty' dollar is almost powerless; or rather, that powerful as it is, it meets with its conqueror in the jealous pride" of the Western settlers.[69] "You see that's the way with us Western folks," Mrs. Kirkland was informed. "If folks is sassy we walk right into 'em, like a thousand o' brick."[70]

Self-importance also fed local prejudices which were directed against those even less fortunate than the poorer Westerners. "Now there a'n't no pride among the Indians," Simeon Jenkins told Mrs. Kirkland; "they all eat out of one dish, and drink out of one bottle. . . . the Indians is nasty creatures. . . . you'll never catch me eatin' with Indians nor niggers. They never were meant to associate with white folks."[71] And she copied from one of Mr. Sibthorpe's letters another Western opinion, the place of Negroes in wilderness society:

"Well!" said Mr. Sibthorpe, with his usual good humor, "I am glad to have met at last with one consistent American. You believe in the equal rights of all human beings. You are not for exalting one class of men at the expense of another, or depressing any class that another may live in pride and luxury at their expense—"

"No indeed!" said our host, with a virtuous severity depicted on his countenance. "Give every man a fair chance, that's what I say; and then we can see what stuff he's made of. Outside, a'n't nothing."

"You are not one of those," continued Mr. Sibthorpe, "who would shut a man out from all the privileges of society because God has given him a black skin. You would look only at his worth, his abilities, or his piety; you would be willing to associate with him, and assist him in maintaining his just natural rights in spite of a cruel prejudice. You would—"

"What upon airth *are* you talking about?" exclaimed our host,

quite aghast at this sweeping conclusion. "I should ra'ally be glad
to know if you mean to insult me! Are you a talking of niggers?
Do you suppose I look upon a nigger as I do upon a white man?
Do you think I am sich a fool as not to know who the Africans
is? Should I put myself upon an equality with the seed of Cain,
that was done over black to show that they was to be sarvants
and the sarvants of sarvants? I'm no abolitionist, thank God! and
if you're one, the sooner you get back to your own country the
better." [72]

Such frankness was disarming, or impertinent, or cruel. Regardless, it was indicative of the Westerners' pride. Farmers and artisans, semiprofessional men and tradesmen—all free and equal—
felt perfectly at liberty to ask questions about any subject or to
offer unsolicited opinions. Westerners, Mrs. Kirkland remarked,
were "every-day, plain people,—men who would 'shake a king by
the hand,' or perhaps 'ask him the price of the throne he sat on,'
without a misgiving;—and women, who, after conning over the
splendors of the young queen's nuptials, [would] talk with majestic
philosophy of 'so much fuss about nothing!' " [73] Her neighbors de-
livered their opinions on the "gimcracks" she had brought from the
East. It was envy that prompted them to speak, but often it was
simply the impractical aspect of having highfalutin "things" on the
frontier. It was their "majestic philosophy" of simplicity that allowed them to say candidly: "pride never did nobody no good." [74]
And it was an irony Mrs. Kirkland could only share with her
readers.

In reporting these "Western peculiarities" of friends and neighbors and in describing with greater understanding "what at first
seemed so odd," Mrs. Kirkland noted their provincialisms, their
customs, their ways of thinking, especially the impact of the
rugged environment on their lives. Life was a struggle for survival
in the Western wilderness, relieved only temporarily by the precious pleasures of idle moments. Life was harsh, often cruel, often
tragic. Indeed, tragedy largely underscored Western life. Yet the
majority of Westerners had a stoical acceptance of conditions and
searched for the home-bred virtues and common incidents which
made life endurable. Independence and initiative, restlessness and
alienation, practicality and simplicity, humor and hospitality—all
were nurtured by the Western wilderness. All were regional characteristics imposed by time and place. Curiously, these regional

characteristics—although they were peculiar to the West in the 1830's and 1840's—have a way of becoming less unique in the passage of time and experience. As Randall Stewart remarked, "The paradox of such . . . provincialism[s] is that [they achieve], without deliberately setting out to do so, the real thing in universality." [75] In emphasizing what were at the time at least Western provincialisms, Mrs. Kirkland pointed the way for the regionalists who were to follow her; her son doubtless read *Forest Life* with profit when he began a generation later his own writing.

V *Western Clearings*

Forest Life was popular enough with her readers, who provided the practical index to Mrs. Kirkland's reputation, so that publishers were willing to contract for another book. She began to think of another volume which she could pull together in the leisure time from her school. Letters to several publishers were written and tentative arrangements were made. "I should wish to know," she wrote Carey and Hart in 1844, "exactly what pieces [you] will [need] to make up the volume. Must they be all *Western?* What title do you propose giving the [book]?" [76] Carey and Hart did not publish *Western Clearings,* however; it was brought out by Wiley and Putnam and was bound in the same volume as Hall's *The Wilderness and the War-Path.* In the preface to the miscellany, Mrs. Kirkland questioned writing still more sketches of Western life "already reported so often," admitting that they might "seem almost like mere repetitions." [77] Mrs. Kirkland's reservations reflected, perhaps, those of her readers and critics.

Western Clearings was patchwork—articles and essays, many of them previously published in magazines, randomly selected and hastily edited. Compared with *A New Home* and *Forest Life,* it was merely hackwork by a woman who knew that her reputation was secure. A kind explanation, probably an accurate one, for such a piece of work is that the Kirklands in the months following their return to New York desperately needed money. Compared with the other two books, *Western Clearings* also set a very different tone. The very real need for money, undoubtedly her own immediate sense of despair at their misfortunes in the West, perhaps her own bitterness—consciously or unconsciously—dictated the choice of material that went into the miscellany. Regardless of reasons, the picture of the West emerging from the book emphasized what was oppressive, embittering, and often ugly in Western life. The regionalist's technique was used again in *Western Clearings:* "to delineate . . . the very ordinary scenes, manners and customs of Western life," but "the 'tie of brotherhood' " was missing.

Although the sketches purported to have a "general . . . correctness," the impression given the reader was that the West was inhabited by a race of cantankerous men: "land-sharks . . . swallowin' up poor men's farms"; inveterate "borrowers"; feuding lovers; ignorant Western nabobs; wrathful litigants; idlers; young women whose "grand desideratum [is] a husband." [78] Westerners, the reader is led to believe, were waspish men, ever on the lookout for a show of false pride in their neighbors:

> As was the accusation of witchcraft in olden times—a charge on which neither evidence, judge nor jury, was necessary to condemn the unfortunate suspected,—so with us of the West is the suspicion of pride—an undefined and undefinable crime, described alike by no two accusers, yet held unpardonable by all. Once established the impression that a man is guilty of this high offence against society, and you have succeeded in ruining his reputation as a good neighbour. Nobody will ask you proof; accusation is proof. This is one of the cases where one has no right to be suspected. The cry of 'Mad dog!' is not more surely destructive.[79]

Yet these same Westerners were themselves vainglorious in their own actions, especially in vying for place—an attitude they had aped from their Eastern neighbors:

> . . . we must laugh when we see the managers of a city ball admit the daughters of *wholesale* merchants while they exclude the families of merchants who sell at *retail;* and still more when we come to the "new country" and observe that Mrs. Penniman, who takes *in* sewing, utterly refuses to associate with her neighbour Mrs. Clapp, because she goes *out* sewing by the day; and that our friend Mr. Diggins, being raised a step in the world by the last election, signs all his letters of friendship, "D. Diggins, Sheriff." [80]

"Hiring-out" was now "loss of caste" in the Western community; and keeping "a school in the country [was] only another name for starvation, and not reputable [genteel] starvation either." [81]

The ideas in the essays were not new, but the emphasis gave a distorted view of Westerners who were primarily a group of peevish eccentrics. Silas Ashburn in "The Bee-Tree" was a shiftless settler whose "bad luck" kept his family destitute, a man like Mr. B—— and like the Newlands in *A New Home.* Mrs. Kirkland implied that it was an ineptitude in the character of some men who came West expecting Eden without working for it or using common sense. Ashburn "had a county to choose from" when he located his farm in a marshy area instead of in the uplands, thereby subjecting himself and his family to attacks of the ague. "Everybody knows if you've got to have the ague, why you've got to, and all the high land and dry land, and *Queen Ann* [quinine] in the world wouldn't make no odds," he argued. Living in the West was hard, and time could not be spent in land speculating or in such "idle" pursuits as hunting or fishing or—as Ashburn preferred—locating bee trees or sending his family out to pick berries in season to sell to farmers who were picking their own. A fiercely struck independence and pride, and his laziness, got in the way of Ashburn's working for other people. Instead of clearing a tract of land for a neighbor who gave him the job because he felt sorry for the family, Ashburn informed him that he could not "begin it today" because he and his sons were looking for a bee tree. "I've got something else that must be done first. You don't think your work is all the work there is in the world, do you?" The irate neighbor echoed Mrs. Kirkland's opinion: "pride and beggary" on the part of settlers like Ashburn plagued the more energetic emigrants to the West, and the problem of getting help in an "operative democracy" was too often an insurmountable one.[82]

Mrs. Kirkland wrote about the problem petulantly. "Mrs. Lowndes['s] . . . forlorn log-house had never known door or window; a blanket supplying the place of the one, and the other being represented by a crevice between the logs. Lifting the sooty curtain with some timidity, I found the dame with a sort of reel before her, trying to wind some dirty, tangled yarn; and ever and anon kicking at a basket which hung suspended from the beam overhead by means of a strip of hickory bark. This basket contained a nest of rags and an indescribable baby; and in the ashes on the rough hearth played several dingy objects, which I suppose had once been babies."

"Is your daughter at home now, Mrs. Lowndes?"

"Well, yes! M'randy's to hum, but she's out now. Did you want her?"

"I came to see if she could go to Mrs. Larkins, who is very unwell, and sadly in need of help."

. . . "Well, I donnow but I would let her go for a spell, just to 'commodate 'em. M'randy may go if she's a mind ter. She needn't live out unless she chooses. She's got a comfortable home, and no thanks to nobody. What wages do they give?"

"A dollar a week."

"Eat at the table?"

"Oh! certainly."

"Have Sundays?"

"Why no—I believe not the whole of Sunday—the children, you know—"

"Oh no!" interrupted Mrs. Lowndes, with a most disdainful toss of the head. . . . "[I]f that's how it is, M'randy don't stir a step! She don't live nowhere if she can't come home Saturday night and stay till Monday morning." [83]

With one exception (Richard Brand in "Bitter Fruits from Chance-Sown Seeds"), the people who inhabited the West in *Western Clearings* were shiftless eccentrics—or such was the view presented. Mrs. Kirkland had talked about such men in *A New Home* and in *Forest Life;* but most Westerners in the other books had been honest, industrious settlers—with delightful quirks and oddities but without the insolent cast she assigned them in *Western Clearings.* "These are *Western* stories," she announced doggedly in the preface, "—stories illustrative of a land that was once an El Dorado—stories intended to give more minute and life-like representations of a peculiar people." [84] The promise of the West had indeed been blighted; "peculiar people"—men like Ashburn and women like Mrs. Lowndes—occupied a wilderness waste.

The tone in *Western Clearings* was little less than amazing. *A New Home* and *Forest Life* had described El Dorado with sympathy and understanding and humor; *Western Clearings* was indeed "bitter fruit." There was a good deal of truth in Hall's blunt statement to his publishers when he heard they were bringing out his book and Mrs. Kirkland's in a single volume: "I beg you not to inflict so great an injury upon me, and so great a disgrace upon my book. The Western Clearings is a wretched composition—a vile piece of humbug. If the authoress was ever in the West, she has failed to convey the slightest idea of the country or its people." [85]

VI   *Character, Language, Style*

Mrs. Kirkland creates, however, two vital characters in these books: Richard Brand in *Western Clearings* and Aunty Parshalls in *Forest Life*. They remind the reader of the delight he shared with the author in so many of the Westerners in *A New Home:* Mr. Ketchum who, after a day's work, took his bottle with him to bed, soon "snor[ing] most sonorously"; the part-time blacksmith Simeon Jenkins whose hankering for public office prompted him to offer himself as a candidate on whichever ticket was more popular; his pipe-smoking sister Cleory, the village schoolmistress, willing to "chore 'round" until school was in session; Mr. Jennings, the practical Westerner, whose candid opinion —"now to my thinkin' "—was usually right; Mrs. Titmouse, with the untamable tongue, "who [could] talk all day without saying anything"; Philo Doubleday, the mild-mannered, soft-spoken villager never at a loss for rhymes that effectively caught the humor in the situation of the moment. Letting these men and women speak and act for themselves, Mrs. Kirkland is always able to catch them in a way that best reflected the human comedy. They are honest, sensible, sometimes admirable people.

Richard Brand may owe something of his character to the Indian-haters whom Hall described in his legends, and something to Natty Bumppo when Cooper moved the old scout to the Western prairies. Like the grandfather in John Steinbeck's "The Leader of the People," Brand has memories of the past more vivid to him than the realities of the present—memories recalling the dangers of Western life and also the humor:

. . . when I first settled, and the Indians was as thick as snakes, so that I used to sleep with my head in an iron pot for fear they should shoot me through the logs, I dug [a] hole and fix'd it just right for 'em, in case they came prowlin' about in the night. I laid a teterin' board over it, so that if you stepped on it, down you went; and there was a stout string stretch'd acrost it and tied to the lock of my rifle, and the rifle was pointed through a hole in the door; so whoever fell into the hole let off the rifle, and stood a good chance for a sugar-plum. I sot it so for many years and never caught an Indian, they're so cunning; and after they'd all pretty much left these parts, I used to set it from habit. But at last I got tired of it and put up my rifle at night, though I sill sot my trap; and the very first night after I left off puttin' my rifle through the hole, who should come along but my own brother from old Kentuck, that I hadn't seen for twenty year! He went into the hole about the slickest, but it only tore his trowsers a little; and wasn't I glad I hadn't sot the rifle?[86]

One of the fullest portraits, and perhaps the most lovable, is Aunty Parshalls—the patient, toiling old woman "with whom the country in general claim[ed] relationship." Saddled with a selfish, exacting, indolent husband and with an indifferent, often imprudent son, she performs a man's and a woman's work around the farm and spins her neighbors' wool to get "hard money." Her concern for her grandson and for her son's young and foolish wife reminds one of Willa Cather's Neighbor Rosicky whose faith in his daughter-in-law encouraged her to respect the homely virtues. Aunty Parshalls' eccentricity is a marvelous "dish-kettle":

. . . It cooked the potatoes for breakfast, and was then put on to heat water for washing the dishes. When this same washing process was about to commence, the dish-kettle was always hoisted to the table, since where was the use of wearing out a pan when the dish-kettle did just as well, and kept the water hot longer too? By the time the dishes were washed, it was time to feed the pigs, and then poor Aunty, being sadly scanted in pails, carried this heavy iron vessel up the rising ground at the top of which the pen was placed. Then the kettle was scoured and put on for dinner. After dinner came the whole dish-washing process over again, and then the factotum was cleaned once more, and put on to heat water for mopping the floor—a daily ceremony. At this point of the diurnal round I confess a discrepancy of opinion between Aunty Parshalls and myself, since I could never quite like to see the mop going in and out of the dish-kettle. But as she said in reply to a very sharp remonstrance of her lady daughter [-in-law] on this head, "Why! bless your dear soul! I sca-oured it!" I will answer for it she did, but we all have our prejudices.[87]

The last view of the old woman is one where she is standing on top of the hill behind the cabin, on the overturned dish kettle, her scantily clad figure in bold relief against the setting sun, looking around the farm with a searching glance. "I do wonder," she thinks, "what has become of that heifer critter. If my old man comes home afore I find her, I shall get an awful talkin' to!" [88]

More often than not, Mrs. Kirkland had the good sense to let Aunty Parshalls and the other Westerners just talk, thereby transmitting the flavor of Western speech. "For to the instructed person," she wrote in the preface to *Western Clearings*, "from one of our great Eastern cities, the talk of the true back-woodsman is scarce intelligible. His indescribable *twang* is, to be sure, no further from good English than the *patois* of many of the English counties. But at the West this curious talker is your neighbor and equal, while in the elder country he would never come in your way unless you sought him purposely to hear his jargon." [89] The frontier dialect helped to stamp the characters' individuality and contributed to the regional flavor of the sketches:

"Hilloa! Steve! where are you a stavin' to? If you're for Wellington, scale up here and I'll give ye a ride. I swan! I'm as lonesome as a catamount! You won't have no objection, I suppose?" turning slightly to Mrs. Margold. The lady did not forbid, and the traveller was soon on the box, much to Mr. Butts's relief, as he now had an interlocutor.

"How do you stan' it nowadays?" was the salutation of Mr. Butts to his friend.

"O, so as to be a crawlin' most of the time. Be you pretty beauty this summer?"

"Why, I'm middlin' tough. I manage to make pork ache when I get hold on't."

"Are you hired with any one now, or do you go on your own hook?"

"I've been teamin' on't some for old Pendleton that built them mills at Wellington. I come on to drive a spell for this here old feller," (jerking his thumb backward,) "but I guess we sha'n't hitch long."

"Why not? Don't he pay?"

"Pay! O, no danger o' that! money's the thing he's got most of. But he wants a *servant*, and that, you know, Steve, is a berry that don't grow on these bushes."

"So he hired you for a servant, eh!" and at the thought "Steve" laughed loud and long.

"Why! a body would think you had found a haw-haw's nest

with a te-he's eggs in't!" said Mr. Butts, who seemed a little
nettled by his friend's ridicule.[90]

*   *   *

"My friends and feller-citizens," said [Simeon Jenkins], self-
sacrificing patriot, "I find myself conglomerated in such a way,
that my feelin's suffers severely. I'm sitivated in a peculiar sitiva-
tion. O' one side, I see my dear friends, pussonal friends—friends,
that's stuck to me like wax, through thick and thin, never shinnyin'
off and on, but up to the scratch, and no mistake. O' t'other side
I behold my country, my bleedin' country, the land that fetch'd
me into this world o' trouble. Now, sence things be as they be,
and can't be no otherways as I see, I feel kind o' screwed into an
augur-hole to know what to do. If I hunt over the history of the
universal world from the creation of man to the present day, I see
that men has always had difficulties; and that some has took one
way to get shut of 'em, and some another. My candid and unre-
fragable opinion is, that rather than remain useless, it is my solemn dooty to change my ticket. It is severe, my friends, but dooty
is dooty. And now, if any man calls me a turn-coat," continued
the orator, gently spitting in his hands, rubbing them together,
and rolling his eyes round the assembly, "all I say is, let him say
it so that I can hear him." [91]

Dialect words—some admittedly "scarce intelligible"—appeared
in the anecdotes and sketches: "lop down" (lie down); "slick up"
or "done off" (dress); "dreen" (drain); "follow the travel" (follow
the road); "flatted out" (failed); "mash" (marsh); "savory cates"
(fried pork and parsnips); "milk emptin's" (home-made bread);
"lightning" (leavening); "reconcilin'" (house cleaning); "keepin'
room" (where entertaining was done). Other idioms suggested a
variety of meanings: "dreadful plaguy"; "lumberin' up"; "clear
grit"; "lettle taunty house"; "a real peeler"; "a little peakin'." Although Mrs. Kirkland was not consistent in her spelling of the
dialect (-*ing*, for example, was just as often -*ing* as it was -*in'*), she
did convey the flavor of the spoken word. Dialect saved a style
which was sometimes too ornamental. Humor often turned on dialect words—when a particular word was used to heighten the ludicrous, when a facetious or ironic twist was wanted for an idea.
Like the regional humorists who employed dialect for similar
ends, Mrs. Kirkland showed facility in the uses of the spoken language.

The moral tone she was to favor in the sentimental tales in *For-*

est Life and *Western Clearings* often resulted, however, in a cumbersome style—not so apparent in the rapidly paced narrative of *A New Home*. In the first book of Western impressions, the relative newness of the material, even the use of idiom which created pictorial phrases, allowed the reader to overlook the moral sentiments. The reviewer in *Graham's* had questioned the frequent use of French words and phrases in *Forest Life;* and it was this "school teacher's knowledge of English, French, Italian, and Latin literature and languages"—as Keyes pointed out—"that most often intruded upon her style and injured it," [92] particularly in the second and third books. Sentences ran to inordinate length; quotations were excessive and the use of irrelevant ones as chapter headings seemed unnecessary. The Western freshness of the style in *A New Home*—so often pure, unrestrained, clear—was largely missing in the later volumes, replaced by a more decorative, a more pedantic, style.

Not only the style but frequently the content of *Forest Life* and *Western Clearings* mark the transition in structure and subject matter to the essays Mrs. Kirkland contributed to the magazines and gift books during the next two decades. *Forest Life* is a valuable document in regional writing because Mrs. Kirkland patiently identifies "Western peculiarities" for the reader. *Western Clearings* is an unsatisfactory picture of the wilderness because Mrs. Kirkland, in a deliberate choice of material, misrepresents the West. The people who live there, according to her "correct" estimate, are dishonest, embittered, shiftless, crafty, cantankerous, and selfish. *Forest Life* describes accurately "what at first seemed odd"; *Western Clearings* is only a regional curiosity.

CHAPTER 4

Union Magazine:
Editor, Contributor, Agent

. . . To *write* is easy, as the immense amount which pours in upon us daily sufficiently evinces; and even to write well, as to style, is not very difficult, as we must think after reading so many happily-expressed pages. But the true point is, to *say something* when we write; to leave a mark on the reader's mind; to give him a new idea, or an old one in a new light; to help his perceptions of truth—whether in morals, manners, art, literature, or whatever else may interest him. In poetry, we hold that a description of sunset, for instance, which does not add a charm to some reader's next view of sunset, is so much paper wasted, *for everybody but the writer*. To him it has a value, and his portfolio is the place for it. The practice of expressing our best thoughts in the best manner we are able, whether in prose or verse, cannot be too highly commended: the wisdom of giving them to the world is more questionable.

—*Union Magazine*[1]

WITH Kirkland's premature death, a severe economic burden was immediately placed on his wife; Mrs. Kirkland was faced with the support of herself and the children solely through her efforts alone. She got more pupils for the school, filled for a time her husband's position in the *Inquirer* office, and went more diligently at the business of writing articles for the magazines. The reputation she had earned with the three books helped immeasurably, of course. And her more influential literary friends—Bryant and the Duyckincks—sent hackwork her way.

To Evert Duyckinck, she sent numerous memorandums during the months after her husband's death—thanking him for favors, soliciting his advice, and asking on one occasion for instructions for correcting proof. She wrote book reviews for *The Literary*

World, demanding anonymity for her work, and was not distressed when Duyckinck edited the material. She was pleased, she told her friend, that she could write longer book reviews for him than she was permitted to do by the editors of the New York *Mirror.* Too often, she complained, the *Mirror* editors "object[ed] to any thing more than a mere notice." [2] Articles under her own name appeared in *Godey's* and the *Columbian*—articles later reprinted in the gift books.

I   *Editor, Contributor, Agent*

Perhaps it was the Duyckincks' influence, or Bryant's, that obtained for her the editorship of a new monthly—*The Union Magazine of Literature and Art.* She wrote Bryant, after she had accepted the position: "I have sole editorial charge— The literary matter will be of course a good deal like that of the other *pictorials,* unless I can contrive to modify it a little in conformity with my own notions of what [it] should be." [3] How successful she was in modifying the "literary matter" to conform to her own tastes, the pages of the magazine reveal. Her aim might well have been a commendable one; for she was concerned—she had written a year or two earlier in the *Democratic Review*—about the "vapid and valueless" fiction appearing in so many magazines, fiction that too often had "nothing to do with this life." She shared her husband's opinion about the extravagant "love tales" published in so many women's magazines; they might be "graceful and pleasant in themselves, but . . . lack[ed] variety and soon pall[ed] the taste." [4] Whatever her private preference might have been, love tales appeared frequently in the *Union*—either to please the women readers or to satisfy the publisher who was, after all, interested in sales. Moreover, she even wrote a number herself.

Love tales, of course, usually concluded with a moral; and such didacticism she certainly approved. Morality in fiction and the essay had much to do with this life. "Nobody has a right, morally speaking, to send forth in print that which has no good aim," she had declared in the article for the *Democratic Review*. And in the "Introductory" which she prepared for the first issue of the *Union,* she stated her position elaborately: "There are more ways than one of exhibiting patriotism. To defend our country when she is attacked, is one which commands the loud applause of the world, and which is therefore the more popular. To elevate the intellectual and moral character of the people, is a work no less necessary and commendable, although far less showy; and this is the aim of the author and the artist. Magazines, though undervalued by the wise, constitute in a country like ours, a powerful element of civilization."

Mrs. Kirkland shared Poe's conviction about the efficacy of magazines: "periodical literature," she continued, "is growing every day upon public favor, as the best possible means of disseminating information, and diffusing the principles of a correct taste. A late writer in Chambers' Journal, proposes that instead of leaving books in the store to be sought for, they should be sent from house to house, in order to insure the greatest benefit from them; and this is just what the cheap monthly magazine can accomplish." [5] And she was greatly annoyed when critics of the *Union* charged that it, like the other women's magazines of the day, was often "filled with nothing but love stories"; she solicited the aid of a friend—perhaps Bayard Taylor in the *Tribune* office—"to defend [the *Union*] from unjust aspersions." [6]

The "content" of the *Union* was, nevertheless, all that the publisher and an appreciative public wanted.[7] Although it published a great many love tales, it also contained excellent prose and poetry as well. Mrs. Kirkland wrote a number of "Western Sketches," none printed previously in *A New Home,* in *Forest Life,* or in *Western Clearings.* Had she been given the opportunity of being solely in charge of the "literary matter," she might have brought greater distinction to the magazine; but Israel Post, the publisher, was a stubborn, irascible employer who dictated the popular tone of the magazine. Mrs. Kirkland had an independent mind, a high degree of intelligence, and an appreciation for literature. Had she been able to make the *Union* the kind of magazine she perhaps envisioned, it might have been a superior periodical—and it probably would not have sold well.

Living "at the West" had taught her a number of obvious lessons, among them the need to be practical at the right time. Had William Kirkland lived, had she not become the breadwinner in the family, she might have exercised her literary inclinations differently—perhaps not. At any rate, she apparently had to compromise literary standards for the magazine with the particular demands of her publisher. She could urge her opinion, but she learned her limits. Post knew Mrs. Kirkland's reputation, and he

insisted that she use her name and position to command contributors to the *Union*. How repugnant doing so was to a sensitive
woman and how often she was chagrined to write letters soliciting
articles, one has no way of knowing. Pressure was probably
brought to bear, although she tried humor to conceal it:

> My publisher [she wrote Bryant] is so truly orthodox that he
> declares we must be saved by a name—and that if I should fill
> the pages of the magazine with the best literary matter that ever
> illuminated type it would be of no use (pecuniarily) if written by
> Tom, Dick and Harry— Now under these circumstances can not
> . . . you come to the rescue in the shape of *one single page* of
> prose? on any conceivable subject—the influence of country life
> —reminiscences of your own early life—of the scenery of your
> native town—characteristics of people about there—changes
> made by the progress of physical improvement—on some subject
> connected with natural science—or the habits of bird or beast—
> I enumerate subjects as they occur to me, hoping to save you
> some trouble in case you think of obliging me—[8]

She wrote Henry Wadsworth Longfellow a similar letter,[9] and to
Taylor she indicated just how insistent Post was: "It is quite an
object with us to obtain known and popular *names* for our Jan.
No—the *quality* of the article is secondary— (This for your private ear as a mem[orandum] from the publisher.)"[10] For the
issue she tried to enlist Willis's support,[11] and E. A. Duyckinck's. "Are you disgusted because I have not been able to make
the magazine more purely literary—" she asked Duyckinck when
he had failed to send an article. "I shall elevate it as fast as I
can. . . . [But] you must help me," she pleaded.[12] Of course,
Mrs. Kirkland's appeals to literary friends were no different from
those of other editors who often had to beg for articles; but the
correspondence only thinly veiled the distasteful fact, to Mrs.
Kirkland at least, that she was prostituting herself in this business
of seeking contributions.

Aside from these letters she had to write, she had her own material to prepare under the pressure of deadlines. "I am working
night and day," she wrote Post (and once again employing a sense
of humor, which must have gotten her through many exasperating
moments), "trying to get *posted* up before I throw all into your
hands. I do not find it easy," she continued, "to write articles

under present circumstances—but will do what I can." [13] The
drudgery connected with preparing copy for the press every
month she grew to detest, referring once to the magazine itself as
the "hateful thing!" after a particularly exhausting work session.[14]
Yet the money she received for the work was desperately needed;
otherwise, she wrote a friend six months after she took the assignment, "I should soon give [it] up." [15]

She convinced Post in the spring of 1848 that she ought to go to
Europe to report the sights and her impressions in articles for the
magazine, and she also persuaded her friend Taylor to assume her
editorial responsibilities until she returned. Taylor received a
number of letters from her during the European trip—letters usually enclosed with "pacquets" of copy sent for publication:

> I send you the first fruits of my flight [she wrote Taylor, just
> after landing in England]—written in all sorts of inconvenient
> ways and places— I beg you will do me the favor to correct the
> whole without scruple, where your taste and judgment sees occa-
> sion. I promise you full impunity, for I have very little literary
> varnish as to small matters, and can bare to have them dealt with
> without gloves. I fear you will not like my random title of Sight-
> seeing—if so, you are at liberty to change or add to it—make it
> more sober or more explanatory as you like— In three weeks or
> so I shall send you another pacquet if we are fortunate.[16]

Mrs. Kirkland's "sight-seeings" were no more distinguished than
were those impressions of so many of her contemporaries who
went abroad and wrote about their experiences. (Emerson's, of
course, would become an exception.) Too often she was simply
the American traveler out to do and to see the things that made
good copy or good talk for impressionable readers or friends at
home. "I am racing through galleries every day," she wrote Taylor, "hoping to learn a little something about pictures. . . . We
are working hard at sight-seeing and lion-hunting—have break-
fasted with [Samuel] Rogers and lunched with Joanna Baillie—
chatted with Dickens in his charming library, and seen him play
Justice Shallow for the benefit of [a] Shakespeare fund. . . ."

Her "budget for the Union," she advised Taylor, would require
careful proofreading. "I am obliged to write by snatches, and . . .
besides, I have hardly read any of it over—that takes too much
time and would not do much good when one's brain is in a fer-

ment with novelties and excitement." [17] Since postage was very expensive, she adopted the somewhat dubious expediency of sending copy to Taylor by American travelers returning home.

After several weeks in England and France, she went on to Italy in June—recording in letters to Taylor at least her momentary disappointment with the country. "[I] cannot get up much enthusiasm about Roman ruins," she confessed, "—most of them being stript of their marbles, appear too much like the brick remains after a fire." She discovered that there were in the city very few residents whom she had hoped to meet, and "not one of all the Americans to whom we brot letters is in Rome." Margaret Fuller was away for the summer; she had written Mrs. Kirkland a note, however, saying that she could not write for the *Union* because she was busy preparing a book about her experiences in Italy. George Duyckinck's letter of introduction to the Robert Brownings in Florence was graciously received, and the meeting between the poets and the editor was "very pleasant." [18] Yet she missed her children and longed to be home again.

When she returned to New York in mid-October, Mrs. Kirkland found that Post had sold the magazine to John Sartain, the engraver who had done many of the "embellishments" for the *Union;* that the editorial office was moved to Philadelphia, where Sartain preferred to live; and that she now had a co-editor, John S. Hart, a teacher in the Philadelphia schools. But Hart, for all intents and purposes, was editor of the monthly; for he informed the readers in January, 1849, that he was happy to have "the services of Mrs. KIRKLAND, who will continue . . . to contribute to [the *Union's*] pages." [19]

In the beginning, the association with Hart and Sartain was an agreeable one. It insured Mrs. Kirkland an income, allowed her some control over material published, and relieved her from much of the editorial routine. Living in New York rather than in Philadelphia made her indeed a contributor much more than an editor; but she did, more frequently and more willingly under Hart, write letters enlisting the literary services of friends and acquaintances.[20] She obviously enjoyed her position; as a talent-seeker, she was often pleased by the confidence writers placed in her. "You must learn to put a price upon yourself," she told James Russell Lowell, who had agreed to submit poems for publication in the *Union.* "I always comfort my modesty when I ask a round sum, by the reflection that the thing has in truth a market value, quite separate and distinct from its claim, as to literature in general— Do you not see that in this view one has only to exercise a little mercantile sagacity—leaving intrinsic appreciation to Apollo, as of old? Shall I ask twenty or twenty-five dollars—or what—for your poem, which I think is charming." [21] She apparently asked twenty dollars, and Lowell—encouraged by her letter—asked thirty dollars. Hart, willing to pay the lower price, was puzzled by Lowell's request. She too expressed surprise at Lowell's demand, exclaiming—one can hardly say, innocently—"Now I believe I *did* nothing—but only suggested." [22]

She was also contributing her own material to the *Union:* more impressions of the tour of Europe, as well as book reviews and essays for the women readers—"homilies," she sometimes called them. She warned Hart that she would need as much time as he could give her in correcting proofs for her articles and admonished him to be sure that the corrections she indicated were in fact made. For a time the editor humored her eccentricities, since she had not been feeling well for several months. She began, however, to object to editing material she herself had solicited and was vexed when her contributors questioned her editing or asked her why their articles were delayed in publication. "They teaze me," she wrote petulantly, "and use my time without benefit." Clearly, she was objecting to an assignment in which she had previously delighted.

Hart, obviously annoyed, in a note at the end of her letter— perhaps addressed to an assistant in the office—scribbled: "We will do no such thing as announce that she is not an editor.— We pay her for being teazed. The old Ladys digestive organs appear to be some what impaired." [23] She grew more demanding, as the months passed, about the careless way in which her articles especially were set in type; and, when she felt that she was being dictated to by the editor and the publisher, she wrote partly in anger and partly in self-pity:

. . . I must say that the general tone of your letter surprises me. I do not know how to reconcile it with what I heard when at Phil.ª a few weeks since. I can make allowance for the vexations and trials of business, but it puzzles me to guess how the same person who so lately said to me that he considered one of the arti-

cles I was furnishing the magazine, worth—I do not remember
how many of Miss Martineau's. Prof. H. made at the same time
the remark that such papers as that on Conversation . . . were
popular and advantageous—an opinion in which the press has
joined on various occasions, not to speak of frequent assurances
on the part of individuals of judgment. . . .

The remark respecting paying $125 for an article on Dress is
most singular. When I give my name to a publication I do not
expect to be subjected to this sort of reckoning. As to "Gossip
from New York"—that is not in my line, and I must beg respect-
fully to decline any attempt of this kind. If my services to the
magazine are not profitable to it I have no desire to force them
upon it. I have done my best, and can do no more. I can neither
write to order as to length nor subject, though I am always willing to oblige as far as my ability will serve. My interest in the
Magazine has been shown by always doing my duty faithfully by
it— I hope I shall never be found unfaithful to my engagements.
In this instance, I have fulfilled them, to the smallest particular. . . .[24]

Little was done to stem the growing antagonism between Mrs.
Kirkland and the *Union* managers. Becoming tired of the association, she was objecting more strongly to conditions which had
previously been agreeable. She had now for a year, by her own
admission, had "too many irons in the fire—writing one book, editing another—besides . . . the Christian Inquirer."[25] She had
been writing book reviews as well for the Duyckincks' *Literary
World,* and she at least offered to write them for Francis Bowen,
editor of the *North American Review.*[26] She could have used another cliché—not wanting to put "all her eggs in one basket"—in
giving her reason for reluctance to work any longer for the Phila-
delphia-based monthly. Fewer signed articles appeared in the
magazine after 1849, although her name was carried as editor
along with Hart's until June, 1851.

II *The Western Sketches*

For the modern reader, Mrs. Kirkland's Western sketches—
eleven in number, which appeared during the years of closest association with the *Union*—have the greatest merit, although these
pieces are uneven in composition.[27] She exhibits once again the
frank delight she found in her Western neighbors in *A New
Home.* The sketches of Western mannerisms are similar to those

in *Forest Life.* "I am told," she wrote a correspondent, "some Western people find fault with my sketches, yet there is a much greater number who confirm your judgment that my pictures are in the main true— The Western people wish to be flattered. Self glorification is the order of the day there—but I will not flatter— though I shall be equally careful not to misrepresent. I love the West, and shall be glad to do it good by telling the truth, even if I get the dislike of some." [28]

In "The Village School," Mrs. Kirkland talked about the eccentric schoolteachers who kept the town's schools. Miss Cynthia Day, "a damsel of few personal charms, and little superfluous learning," was simply incompetent; Mr. Hardcastle, "a sober and down-looking" divinity-school student who was "too delicate in mind and body" for the frontier, did not last the term because he could not control the wilder boys. Miss Pinkey was the disciplinarian, who developed such ingenious "instrument[s] of torture" that everybody—parents included—was glad when winter "gave an opportunity to dismiss so efficient a teacher." Mr. Ball was merely a "blusterer, who was more intent on impressing . . . [the villagers] with a high idea of his personal consequence, than in performing the duties expected of him." Only Miss Wealthy Turner "kept her ground" with the pupils and pacified the parents, thus "vindicat[ing] her authority by such strictness in school, that offences gradually became less frequent, and the interests of learning advanced accordingly." [29] Mrs. Kirkland created an amusing sketch, yet the reader inferred how irritating it was to a teacher to have such ill-prepared teachers often in charge of Western schools. The sketch doubtless suggested something about Western schools to her son Joseph when he wrote about Anne Sparrow, his schoolteacher in *Zury: The Meanest Man in Spring County* (1887).

"Harvest," as the title implied, evoked descriptively the season of the year; Mrs. Kirkland listed the delights of rural life at harvest time. The essay was a reworking of an earlier essay, "Harvest Musings," which had appeared first in *Knickerbocker's* and then was reprinted in *Western Clearings.*

"The Justice" was a series of vignettes dealing with the miscarriages of justice in a raw, new country—a topic she had written about in *A New Home.* She suggested in this sketch, as she had in *A New Home,* that litigation was often regarded by Westerners as a kind of popular amusement: "mere animal excitement—nay, even the rousing of the angry and destructive passions, is preferred to apathy." Speaking frankly, she admitted that too often the ignorant farmer who became a justice was wooed by the litigant who courted him. As a result, "decisions are often so monstrously unjust and improper," she declared, "that the whole public voice cries out at once against them; in which case a new trial is inevitable, and more loss of time and money, more ill-blood, and more disappointment follow, both parties growing more angry as the dispute proceeds. . . . Testimony, in bringing forward new points, brings up old grievances; treachery is developed, party feelings are raised, family secrets dragged to light;—and the end of all is, too often, sorely-wounded feelings, life-long enmity, and perhaps secretly-nourished schemes of revenge." Frequently, litigation was prompted by "a mean, unscrupulous class of lawyers"—emigrants from the East—who came to this "land of golden promise for adventurers" and incited the ignorant, the unwary, or the wretched to file for absurd claims.[30] Although she had been largely amused by the antics of her Western neighbors anxious to go to the law in *A New Home*, she castigated the Westerners in this sketch for submitting to such unprincipled practices. Here she more closely than in the other Western sketches in the *Union* adopted the tone of the sketches in *Western Clearings*.

The incident in "The Country Funeral" was no more typically Western than any similar experience in a rural, or suburban, area where people become "active, useful, quiet friend[s]" to the bereft family. However, the incident in "Steps to Ruin" was not peculiar to the frontier alone; it was simply a tract on the evils of drinking. The sentiments in both these sketches were particularly feminine expressions, as agreeable for Mrs. Kirkland to write as for her female contemporaries to read. "Steps to Ruin" was later added to a series of "Recollections of Rural Life in the West" prepared for *A Book for the Home Circle*.

"The Singing School" and "A Love of a Singing Master" were companion pieces—a tale of a singing master in the village who was exposed as an errant husband. He had wooed one of the girls in the village who had accompanied him and his choir to a quarterly church meeting. There he met his wife who had also come to sing. The two sketches were combined into one story under the title, "The Singing School," which was published later in *The Evening Book.*

"The Hard Winter" described the privations brought about by a summer drought, a rainless fall, a snowless winter—when streams and wells on the farms dried up and men and cattle nearly starved. "The only traffic of the district, for a time," Mrs. Kirkland related, "was the sale of hides; and flour had become so scarce and dear from the stopping of the mills, that the pittance realized on the poor remains of the cattle that had helped raise the grain, would hardly buy a week's bread! . . . The straw-covering of the sheds was all pulled off and eaten, and it was not uncommon for men to be all day employed in cutting down young maples in the woods, that their cattle might browse upon tender branches. The general sadness was indescribable, for what touches the farmer's cattle touches his life." The message in the brief sketch—only a page in length—is masterfully understated; the language is terse; the warning is blunt. Eden can become an arid wasteland, and man is caught in the grip of a relentless nature. In a very few words she outlines a real horror for the pioneer who often gambled comfort and his own welfare on the promise of the West. Woe to the faint of heart, Mrs. Kirkland advised: "They have nothing to do at the West. They must fly or die!" [31]

She argued a rather convincing case for "Sunday in the Country" as being uniquely a Western experience. Sunday was apparently different—"a day of *rest,* emphatically; and a day of cleanliness, and dress, and social congregation, and intellectual exercise; and perhaps of reading and reflection, such as the toilsome week-days do not encourage." And great stillness prevailed—none of the noise, the boasting, the bravado which marked the Westerners' lives the other days of the week. Many went to church, but many did not. Mrs. Kirkland admired greatly "these independent people [who] say, 'It is a free country, and every man can do as he likes'[;] they do not claim the least right to interfere with a neighbor's freedom. That would not be tolerated by any one." [32] Her Western neighbors gossiped and borrowed and held opinions contrary to her own; but she appreciated the freedom they often gave her, never interfering with her right to be different if she preferred.

In "Forest Literature," really a misleading title, her comments on public education were not only applicable to the West. As a

schoolteacher herself, she was distressed by the public apathy toward education and the lack of support communities so often dis-
played toward teachers.[33]

"The Log-House" described the first home her family had in the
Michigan wilderness. Although a general impression of the cabin
had been reported in *A New Home,* this sketch in the *Union* gave
the details of the rude construction of the Kirklands' wilderness
home.[34] The description was inserted in a story entitled "A Wedding in the Woods," which was published later in *The Evening
Book*—an account of a courtship, a rural wedding, and the
thwarted efforts of the young man's friends to give him and his
bride a Western *"charivari."* The story had appeared first in
Godey's.

Two more sketches, "Bush-Life" and "The Log School-house,"
were printed in the *Union* after Mrs. Kirkland was no longer so
closely associated with the magazine. "Bush-Life" related what
was doubtless Mrs. Kirkland's own "waking-up" to the reality of
living on the frontier. Since she wrote the sketch with the advantage a few years gave in being removed from the experience itself,
she frankly admitted her own "disabilities"; and, in doing so, she
revealed perhaps why her neighbors were sometimes "put out"
with her "fastidiousness":

> Emigrants are apt, at the outset, to feel somewhat of reforming
> zeal. They have just left regions where life wears a smooth as-
> pect; where convention hides much that is coarse and unpleasant.
> . . . So the emigrant feels as if he had much to tell; something to
> teach, as well as something to learn. If he must depend somewhat
> on his neighbors for an insight into the peculiar needs of his new
> position, he is disposed to return the favor by correcting, both by
> precept and example, some of the awkward habits, the ear-
> wounding modes of speech, and unnecessary coarseness which he
> sees about him. Above all does he determine that the excellent
> treatise on farming which he has studied and brought with him,
> shall aid him in introducing, before very long, something like a
> rational system, instead of the short-sighted, slovenly, losing,
> hand-to-mouth practices which are wasting the riches of the land.
>   The waking-up is quite amusing. To find that nobody perceives
> his own deficiencies, while everybody is taking great pains to
> make yours apparent; that your knowledge is considered among
> your chief disabilities; that you are, in short, looked upon as a
> pitiable ignoramus, stuffed only with useless fancies, offensive

pride, silly fastidiousness, and childish love of trifles; that your farming theories are laughed at, and your social refinements viewed as indicating a sad lack of common sense and good feeling. . . . [C]oming from a land where head is all-powerful and hand only subservient, your muscles are feeble and your brain active, you must be content with the position of an inferior, and for awhile play the part of a child in the hands of older and wiser people.

This aspect of Bush-life lacks the pleasant stimulants with which the imagination is apt to invest it. Where are the hunting and fishing which were to cheer your leisure hours? You have no leisure hours; and if you had, to spend them in hunting and fishing would set you down at once as a "loafer"—the last term of condemnation where everybody works all the time; lives to work rather than works to live. Your fine forest dreams give way before the necessity for "clearing." If you take a morning walk over the breezy hills, it will probably be in search of a stray cow; and you may find it necessary to prolong your stroll indefinitely, returning, under the blazing sun of noon, to dinner instead of breakfast. Your delightful, uninterrupted evenings, where so many books were to be devoured, in order to maintain a counter-influence to the homely toils of the day, must be sacrificed, perhaps, to sleep, in order to be ready for an early start in the morning, in search of additional "hands" at the threshing, or that most valuable and most slippery of all earthly goods in the new country—a "hired girl." If you chance to have an old friend undergoing a similar probation ten or twenty miles off, and feeling a yearning desire to seek counsel or sympathy at his hands, be sure that after you have made up your mind to sacrifice everything to this coveted visit, which you feel will set you up in courage for a month to come, you will find you "cannot have the horses," without such a derangement of the business at home as would bespeak an insane disregard of your interest, and lead your whole dependency to look upon you as a fool past praying for.[35]

"The Log School-house" was devoted primarily to a discussion of backwoods religion—the schoolhouse, of course, serving as the church on Sundays. She spoke of the self-appointed, ignorant, itinerant lay preachers who moved about the frontier, "behind those they teach in general intelligence, and not much above them in familiarity with religious topics, though they may possess a great flow of words, which pass for signs of ideas." The logic of their sermons defied close examination, "mere strings of Scriptural phrases and well-known texts, often curiously wrenched from their authorized meaning to favor the purpose of the hour." It was sufficient for the preacher's purpose if the congregation was "touched, moved, excited, frightened, or persuaded into an interest in religion, by any and every means that the Scriptures afford." Although Mrs. Kirkland might not approve of evangelical religion practiced on the Michigan frontier, she willingly admitted its "good" effect on the unsophisticated Westerner. "The best touchstone of valuable citizenship [education and religion] is found in the log school-house." [36] Both sketches reappeared in *The Evening Book*.

Even though some of the sketches do not relate distinctively Western experiences and are simply easy copy for the editor to write, several do contain evaluations of the wilderness life written objectively from the vantage point only distance can give. Others describe in the regionalist's terms frontier types—the schoolteachers, the preachers, the justices—as she had done in *Forest Life*. Unwilling to "flatter," yet equally reluctant to "misrepresent," she avoids censure in the sketches by giving only "likenesses," not individualized portraits as she had done in *A New Home*. However, the Western sketches in the *Union* do not enlarge the reader's vision of Mrs. Kirkland's West; they simply help to fill out her impression of it.

III *Literary Ephemera*

Mrs. Kirkland's essays on her trips to Europe—first in 1848, again in 1850—are often pedestrian in style and content, despite Hart's opinion in the pages of the *Union* that they were "spirited sketches of life abroad, and discriminating notices of whatever in European countries would be likely to interest an educated American." [37] They are what the essay titles indicate—"sight-seeing in Europe"—a collection of impressions gathered from "a flying tour of observation" and the guidebooks. They give the tourist's view of Europe; rarely is Mrs. Kirkland the perceptive commentator Emerson was to be in *English Traits*. The essays are chatty fare: she writes about the discomforts of travel, shopping, fashions, street urchins, and European women. All are dished up agreeably enough for the women readers of the *Union*. Perhaps the only striking feature of the series is her insistent Americanism.

The first tour commenced in Liverpool, where she crossed country to London; then to Paris, where she arrived just after the revolution and the expulsion of Louis-Philippe; by private coach to Genoa, Florence, and Rome and north again to western Germany and the Low Countries. Although Liverpool was, she wrote, "usually described as very uninviting," the city seen through "unprejudiced eyes" had charm, even magnificence, stability and comfort. "Many of the stores," she informed her women readers, "exhibit great exterior elegance, and a closer examination proved that in many departments their supply of splendid and costly articles is no whit behind that of the best establishments in New-York." The Liverpool she saw with its "magnificent docks" and "tall Flemish-looking warehouses" was a very different city from the one Melville had seen some years earlier, for the day was sunny when she was there, making everything seem "soft and beautifying." [38]

Mrs. Kirkland's essay on the stopover in Coventry was largely devoted to good-natured complaining about accommodations:

> We asked for a fire, and after some little time we got smoke.
> . . . We were truly desirous of breakfast, and after some explanations and bell-pullings, and apologies, it came in by instalments [*sic*]; so that by the time we had eaten the bread we got the butter, and the coffee had not become entirely cold before a minute quantity of cream was furnished to soften it with. The maid-of-all-work who waited on us, (we returned the favor by waiting on her,) apologized, saying the servants had been at a ball until four in the morning; and we secretly concluded that her story must be true, for we were quite sure our table-cloth was the one which had served at their supper. But a Coventry breakfast is soon dispatched, so we made our way to the railroad station in good time, scarcely waiting to admire the really pretty old town as we passed. It is wonderful, that a bad breakfast can so starve out one's romance; but all we shall remember of Coventry will be our many resolutions of never sending any of our friends there.[39]

In London, she saw the Queen riding through Hyde Park; "[s]he seemed to us much plainer in every respect than any picture of her we had seen. Her complexion is far from clear, her figure diminutive, her dress devoid of taste." [40] In writing of the English people, she made those casual observations already many times identified as particular characteristics; yet she was able to turn the observations into a favorable comment on her own coun-

trymen. "What a headlong, shifting, mercurial, impulsive, imita-
tive, unfinished people we seem to be, compared with the steady,
reasonable, stolid, self-complacent English, who, having been a
thousand years busily engaged in discovering the best way of doing everything, are quite sure they have found it." It was this attitude of mind—"this obvious self-sufficiency and prejudice"—
which most annoyed Americans. "Our consciousness of defi-
ciency," she wrote, "and willingness to learn, drives us into servile
imitation, and a disposition to think whatever is new must be an
improvement upon the old. Yet the English are evidently, in spite
of themselves, imbibing something of the American spirit, which
we take to be the spirit of this age." Nevertheless, as she counseled
her readers, "let us hope that we shall settle into whatever is good
and stable of the olden *regime*." [41]

Paris was "dull"—understandably, if one remembered the recent revolution. "Scarcely any private equipages are seen in the
streets," she reported, "and very few well-drest people." To Mrs.
Kirkland's mind, the city was hardly a center of fashion. Although
the shops were "abundantly supplied with the most elegant articles," she saw "none which compared in magnificence with some
at home." A Protestant bias often crept into her observations
about Catholic priests and about the Catholic religion: "Many of
the [priests'] faces we happened to see were dull if not gross, and
the manner of performing the services was truly melancholy, so
devoid of all unction and earnestness. . . . We did not happen
upon any grand religious ceremony." [42]

En route to Italy, she passed through Lyons, whose "vileness
can hardly be described in exaggerated terms"—where the "re-
markably ugly" women of the city walked about the streets "as
much at ease without bonnets as if they had been in their own
houses." The only "sweet thing" in the streets was "the music of
two poor little wandering Italian boys, the youngest hardly bigger
than Tom Thumb, who, with each a violin, came and sang and
played . . . like errant angels. They are probably submerged
now." The hotel where she stayed was a "gloomy" building where
"one sees as many shadows, and hears as many suspicious noises,
in such a rambling old place, as the heroines of Mrs. Radcliff's
[*sic*] novels used to do." [43]

The "diligence" she and her traveling companions hired for the
trip into Italy was, she informed her readers, "most impractic-

able." "There seemed nothing but caves behind one's head, nothing but sharp ridges to lean one's elbow upon—an aching void, where the floor, or a footstool ought to have been. We swayed and nodded like wind-swept dahlias; our heads were too large for our necks; and if we slept, it was to dream of running against stone walls or stepping off precipices." In Genoa, they visited the "pink jail" where Dickens had once been lodged. And Mrs. Kirkland was prompted to characterize the novelist as a man whose "naughty things he has said about our country, have not been sufficient to abate our admiration of his genius, and of the excellent aim of his works." [44] She came to enjoy Italy—the country and the people. Even though the descriptions read too often as if she was paraphrasing her guidebook—"We know the rocks were marble beautiful, gold-veined, purple—(*vide*, Murray,) and this made their very outline more exquisite" [45]—she did convey in some of the essays a delight in scenes the guidebook did not include.

"Children play about," she explained, "with multitudes of dogs and cats,—always abounding most where there is least to eat,—and the whole scene is a compound of good humor and dirt, most amusing to witness. Indeed, when one thinks upon the sharp creaking tones and red noses of some over-neat [American] housewives, who feel it a duty to make every life within their influence a sacrifice on the altar of cleanliness, and then upon the gay softness of these easy Italians, who evidently are philosophers with regard to dirt, one is in danger of a doubt as to which has chosen the wiser part." [46] She showed feminine prudishness at times when she gazed at nude sculpture in the galleries of Italy, but she was often deeply impressed. "I wish you could have enjoyed with me the galleries of the Vatican, where all the beauty that earth ever knew seems congregated in imperishable marble," she wrote a friend.[47]

But admiration for Vatican art did not carry over to admiration for the religion which the Vatican symbolized. She witnessed a mass at St. Peter's and, though impressed by the ceremony itself, wrote guardedly to her friend Taylor about the service:

We have been this morning to hear the Pope say mass—one of the three *very* great occasions of the year—the service performed in Greek as well as Latin—three mortal hours of dull music—al-

ways excepting the moment of the elevation of the Host at the
grand altar by the Pope, to the sound of trumpets, when the immense multitudes knelt on the pavement, and the Santo Padre,
who is a most dignified person, raised the golden cup above his
head again and again. It was a scene I shall never forget. The
cardinals and bishops were all present in their most gorgeous
robes—the household troops the Swiss guard and the civic guard
in full uniform, and a great congregation of people, priests, monks
and ladies, to say nothing of the great unwashed.[48]

The Catholic religion was to Mrs. Kirkland—as it was to many of
her contemporaries—a ceremony, elaborate and dignified; but she
had a Protestant suspicion of Catholics, not understanding and
thereby not appreciating the mass, often allowing prejudice to
color her opinion of Catholics themselves.[49]

The travel essays in the *Union* stopped with Mrs. Kirkland's
first impressions of Italy. Whether her packets of manuscript
which she sent Taylor by Americans returning home miscarried,
whether Post in his "mischief" kept them, whether she decided to
withhold installments for her own book, no one knows; nor is it
perhaps important to know. The women who subscribed to the
Union would read her book if they were pleased with the gossipy
content of the essays which had appeared in the magazine; the
modern reader has that choice as well.

In several essays in the *Union* Mrs. Kirkland discussed English
impressions of Americans and English and American manners.
"Detached Thoughts about England" began mildly enough—indeed, the beginning was somewhat reminiscent of Washington
Irving's approach in "English Writers on America" in *The Sketch
Book*. Yet Mrs. Kirkland soon discarded the friendly tone and bus-
tled with womanly (and American) indignation at English superiority:

. . . social England looks upon her American children with con-
tempt only half veiled; prizes not their love, scorns their admiration, views their efforts at improvement with a loft[y] disdain,
studiously avoids recognizing their claims to respect. Arrogating
to herself a superiority that is never to be questioned, she cannot
forgive our showing in her presence any other quality beside
docility. If we come as mere learners; if we begin with an acknowledgment of hopeless inferiority; if we are willing to allow
that to differ from England in any particular, important or trifling,

is to be wrong—she will look upon us with a certain sort of com-
placency; abate a little of her superciliousness, and acknowledge
that we are not quite irredeemably benighted. But even then, the
good sense which perceives English infallibility is considered
rather as an individual exception. America—the vague, disagre-
able [*sic*] something which universal England means by that
word—still lies in darkness, at an unmeasurable distance; despis-
ing dignities; wild after every kind of unrespectable novelty in
politics and religion; abetting all sorts of revolutions; repudiating;
self-glorifying; stealing English books; loving slavery for the pleasure of flaying slaves; chewing tobacco; eating eggs out of wine
glasses! [50]

Many reasons for this anti-American feeling she specified, of
course, in this passage; but the resentment the English felt most
strongly was, in her opinion, America's "material greatness." [51]

In "English and American Manners" she openly praised American democracy, equality, character; like Cooper and a number of
other American writers, she decried the habit of imitating the
English because that way of life was *not* the American way. "The
true glory of the American . . . at home or abroad, is simplicity,
truth, kindness, and a strict regard for the rights and feelings of
others." And she admonished her women readers—so many of
them anxious to copy English manners—not to discount the simple and proud heritage which was theirs alone.[52] The sentiments
she expressed in the essay she felt were significant enough to bear
repeating; so she published it again a few years later, under the
title "What Shall We Be?" in *The Evening Book.*

The other contributions under her name to the *Union* were rela-
tively inconsequential, except a two-part essay on New York.
There were tasteful estimates of Goethe (written after reading
Parke Godwin's translation of the autobiography) and Mahomet
(with due acknowledgment to Irving for information and inspiration); essays on George Sand whom she did not like, largely for
being unfeminine; "Thoughts on Education"—subtitled, "Addressed to Young Women Who Are 'Finishing' "—filled with
teacherly advice on the necessity of knowing "the proprieties."

The essays on "New York" were Mrs. Kirkland's last contributions to the *Union.* She began them with a "history" of the city:
citing statistics, identifying landmarks, naming parks and ave-
nues. She then commented at length on the New Yorkers' "puritan

tone of manners" and lack of "social graces," ones so distinctive in
European society. Money was frequently an index to social position. "No *pose* has yet been attained," she believed, "and each
[person] is too much absorbed in making good his claim to consideration, to have leisure for the enjoyments which might be
snatched during the contest." [53]

> If we should venture to suggest what it is that New York so-
> ciety most lacks, we should say Courage;—courage to enjoy and
> make the most of individual tastes and feelings. The spirit of
> imitation robs social life of all that is picturesque and poetical.
> Living for the eyes of our neighbors is stupefying and belittling;
> it gives an air of hollowness and tinsel to our homes, stealing even
> from the heartiness of affection, and sapping the disinterested-
> ness of friendship:—it tends to the general impoverishment of
> home-life, the privacy of which is the soil of originality, and the
> nursery of accomplishments:—it is hardly consistent with the
> pursuit of literature or art for its own sake; since a desire to do
> what others do, and avoid what others contemn, excludes private
> and independent choice, except where the natural bias is inevit-
> ably strong. There is, in truth, very little relish for home accom-
> plishments in New York. With many honourable exceptions,
> Music is too much a thing of exhibition, and Drawing is scarcely
> practised at all. Two or three of the modern languages are taught
> in every school; but the use of these is seldom kept up in after life,
> even by reading. No people are so poorly furnished with foreign
> tongues as the Americans, and New York forms no exception to
> the general remark.[54]

Mrs. Kirkland's strictures on New York come as a surprise since
she and her friends certainly assisted in establishing the "tone" of
the city's society—her own "finishing" schools, her literary soirees,
her musical entertainments, even her less obvious pursuits of culture such as reading, writing, and conversing. She had recently
returned from the second trip abroad, an extended sojourn in
London and Paris principally; and perhaps her "remarks" were
colored by the cultural advantages these cities offered a well-
educated woman. But the essays on New York are unlike anything
else Mrs. Kirkland wrote; she is not usually outspoken unless there
is reason or justification for the comment, either in her private
convictions or in response to injury assumed or real. Here there
seems to be no cause for the opinions expressed as she adopts the

pose of Cooper in *Home as Found.* Humor is edged too sharply
with ridicule; frankness is armed too heavily with blunt abuse.
Even the style is unlike her conversational, informal approach to
the essay. There is a falseness, even a sophistication (she em-
ploys British spellings, for instance), which makes the style as
artificial as the sentiments it expresses.

IV *Her Contributors to the Union*

One of Mrs. Kirkland's responsibilities was to enlist contributors
to the *Union;* and, while she was editor, she counted among her
authors for the magazine the most popular, and many of the more
significant, writers of the day—Mrs. Lydia H. Sigourney, Mrs.
Lydia M. Child, Miss Catharine M. Sedgwick, Mrs. Sarah H. Os-
good, Mrs. Anne L. Botta, Frederika Bremer, and Harriet Martineau whose stories and essays were immensely popular with
women readers; John Neal, Park Benjamin, Hoffman, Richard
Henry Stoddard, Taylor, Henry T. Tuckerman, E. A. Duyckinck,
Willis, Griswold, George H. Boker as well as, at that time, the
lesser known literati; and William Gilmore Simms, Bryant, Longfellow, and Lowell. Walt Whitman contributed a sentimental tale,
"The Shadow and the Light of a Young Man's Soul"—a sketch of a
youth who worked to overcome inveterate laziness. Thoreau sub-
mitted "Ktaadn, and the Maine Woods," published in five installments, beginning in the summer of 1848. Poe sent in a number of
poems; and after his death, Mrs. Kirkland—no longer editor in her
own name—persuaded Hart to publish an early version of "The
Bells."

The Bells.—A Song.

The bells!—hear the bells!
The merry wedding bells!
The little silverbells!
How fairy-like a melody there swells
From the silver tinkling cells
Of the bells, bells, bells!
Of the bells!

The bells!—ah, the bells!
The heavy iron bells!
Hear the toiling of the bells!
Hear the knells!

How horrible a monody there floats
From their throats—
From their deep-toned throats!
How I shudder at the notes
From the melancholy throats
Of the bells, bells, bells—
Of the bells—[55]

Later, "The Poetic Principle from the Unpublished Manuscript"
and "Annabel Lee" were also published.[56] She was anxious to
establish and then maintain a literary tone for the magazine and
therefore discouraged essays on economics and politics.[57] She was
besieged with "effusions" from aspiring authors; and, finding it
impossible to publish, even to read, them all, she often inserted
notes to her "correspondents" in issues of the magazine when filler
was needed: "We do not think it necessary to publish a list of
rejected articles, as all which are not accepted are left with the
publisher to be called for, in case the owners wish them returned.
To write a letter in every case, as some of our correspondents
seem to expect, is out of our power. We should need two or three
amanuenses for such a labor." [58]

V Book Reviews

As it was, she could have used "two or three amanuenses," for
being an editor was time-consuming, often arduous. In addition to
preparing her own essays, writing contributors, reading and correcting proof, and supplying editorial miscellany, she wrote a
number of book reviews when she alone was editor. They were
not outstanding—perhaps because she lacked critical acumen,
which she readily admitted, or perhaps because her readers were
primarily concerned whether or not a book would appeal to them.
The reviews exhibited feminine sentiment, politely phrased, expressing admiration for the man and his work. Often she had, in
fact, very little to say: "These 'outflowings' of Mr. Emerson," she
wrote in a review of the *Essays*, "are already so well-known—that
is, what is known of them is so well-known—that any attempt of
ours to analyze or to commend them would be impertinent or
useless. We must refer the reader to many learned disquisitions
upon Mr. Emerson and his peculiar genius, to be found in various
reviews." [59]

With someone less formidable than Emerson, she felt more

comfortable. Speaking of Longfellow's *Evangeline,* she pitched
the review specifically to her women readers: "The moral is a high
one—most delicately wrought out, and the story is evolved with
such artistic skill, that although it keeps us trembling on the verge
of tears throughout, it is not until the last line that they rush forth
unbidden." For the benefit of the readers, she included a number
of excerpts from the poem—standard procedure for many reviewers, and in Mrs. Kirkland's case a fortunate one since she was then
not called on to be critical. She concluded the review: "we are not
in the mood to judge very critically of hexameters. We have read
the poem twice through, and it leaves a sweet echo—of that we are
sure, though it has some defective lines—defective in measure, we
mean—as well as a good many prosaic ones. But we will leave it
to somebody else to pull the rose to pieces and discourse botani-
cally upon it." [60] With the feminine writers, she was usually sympathetic, writing enthusiastic reviews of the sentimental tales that
the women novelists and short-story writers were supplying their
readers with.

When an author came closer to what Mrs. Kirkland herself had
attempted in her writing, she had a common understanding and
was better able to evaluate the work. The feminine impulse to
turn a polite phrase was present, but some perception was apparent as well. Her review of *Kavanagh* was appreciative not only of
Longfellow's "peculiar moral encouragement which [the book]
every where impart[s] . . . almost every page teem[ing] with
the spirit of hope, perseverance, and endurance" but of the realistic touches Longfellow worked into the delineation of village life:
"a gallery of the most delightful pictures . . . landscapes . . .
domestic scenes . . . characters." She detected something of the
freshness in the village sights that she had caught in *A New
Home.* A book from the "hand of a great master," *Kavanagh*
would be remembered by readers as the "choicest of choice
books." [61]

With Lowell too she was discerning in a review of the *Poems:*

A tinge of mysticism, not to say mistiness, was discoverable in his
earlier poetry. . . . But the poems in the present volume, at least,
are not liable to this objection. They lay hold stoutly on this lower
world, lifting its hopes and fears and efforts and aspirations to a
spiritual level, from which aupyrean [*sic*] heights may be dis-

cerned, and breath for boundless soaring gained. There is a tone
of deep interest in human affairs; sharp indignation against op-
pression and all moral wrong; earnest recognition of the holy and
the good. The crying sins of the time are handled unsparingly,
and the duty of the poet as prophet, made to appear no whit behind his office as priest of the beautiful.[62]

She told Hart later that Lowell's "A Fable for Critics" was "capital" satire, "so good natured that one can afford to be delighted
with its pungency." [63] She discovered in Lowell two qualities her
own best writing had—moral sentiment and effective satire.

Surprisingly, she was enthusiastic about Melville's early books
in her reviews for the *Union* of *Typee, Mardi,* and *Redburn.* Like
a number of her fellow reviewers, she was pleased to see the
American editions of *Typee* improved with "the omission of certain
parts relating to Tahiti and the Sandwich Islands, which in their
original form gave much discontent, without being at all necessary to the completeness of the narrative." She obviously enjoyed
the expurgated edition, commenting that Melville had "a knack
[for] getting up an adventure as well as of telling it" and regarding *Typee* as "one of the choicest collections of adventure
extant." [64] Adventure and romance provided the attraction in
Mardi, but she was silent about the satiric intent of the novel.
Perhaps the satire puzzled her; perhaps she, like other reviewers,
thought that it was a bad book but was reluctant to condemn it
because of admiration for the author.

We should not be at all surprised to see Polynesia, with its
myriad islands and its bewitching climate, becoming to romance
what the "fabled East" has been for more than thirty centuries.
Magnetism and steam, the railroad and the newspaper, are fast
stripping the East of its solemn mystery. Romance, as well as em-
pire, it seems must travel westward. There is indeed no end to the
illusions with which an active fancy may invest the vast Continent of Islands that lies outstretched in the great Pacific Ocean.
Such is the feeling which rises spontaneously as we close Mr.
Melville's book. We take the feeling as evidence either that he has
been happy in his choice of a subject, or that he has the still
higher merit of having produced from an indifferent subject a
very entertaining work. In either case, we shall be happy to accompany the author in any future voyage he may make in the
same direction.[65]

She felt that Melville had returned to safer harbor in *Redburn,* once again liking the "wild, fascinating spirit of adventure" infusing the book. She acknowledged the tongue-in-cheek manner which Melville employed in writing half the book at least: "His pranks whether among the parts of speech, or on the deck of a brig, are such as bring their own forgiveness in the very breath that says 'the graceless scamp!'" An original writer, "a law to himself," Melville was, in Mrs. Kirkland's estimation, "refreshing in this age of stereotyping and fac-similes [*sic*]"—an author "so unique, so perfectly individual." [66] Her opinion of Melville was not shared by many of her women readers. There was in the younger author a streak of independence, stubborn determination, and frankness of expression which she could appreciate; his impudence—provoking to soberer natures—was reminiscent of a similar tone in the best of her Western writing.

She and her children also admired *White Jacket,* as a note to an editor indicated: "I was on the point of sending White Jacket home and saying that I had no time to look it over—but a few glances showed me that it was such a capital thing, and the young people seized upon it with such avidity—that I had not the heart. So here is my notice, which I could easily have extended, but that I know 'lengthiness' is deprecated in these matters. You shall have the book when you want it—and I advise you to read it." [67] The note was written several days after the Duyckincks had praised *White Jacket* so highly in *The Literary World;* otherwise, one is tempted to assign the reviews of the novel to Mrs. Kirkland. Her later association with Charles F. Briggs and *Putnam's,* however, was no doubt instrumental in helping Melville to place his short stories in that magazine.[68]

When her association with the *Union* ended, Mrs. Kirkland did free-lance writing for other magazines—stories heavy in sentiment and essays of "moral instruction." She wrote no more Western sketches, for she was content with reprintings of *A New Home* and the shorter sketches in the gift annuals. Her vein of Western material had been exhausted—a rich vein while it lasted but not a deep one. Had she the time, she might have done more work, perhaps even better work; but writing and editing for ready money, and teaching for it as well, kept her from more satisfying literary work. Yet she could take comfort in the fact that a host of writers for the magazines had followed her lead and had sent stories about the West to editors anxious to receive them. And she began an interest in regional writing that was to achieve a singular status in American literature in the years following the Civil War. For this pioneer effort alone, she deserves to be long remembered.

CHAPTER *5*

Miscellaneous Writings

THE 1840's and 1850's were the productive years for Mrs. Kirkland, for her continuing popularity with readers gave her the opportunity of compiling a number of gift books, made up of selections from her writings during the preceding years. There is little in these annuals to commend them to the close attention of the reader; but they indicate, of course, that Mrs. Kirkland's reputation was in no way diminishing. The collections—three in number—were designed to win the approval of younger readers as well. Hawthorne's comment about the "d——d mob of scribbling women" was particularly pertinent to a writer like Mrs. Kirkland; for the annuals were serious competition to authors in America who wanted to win popular approval. Indeed, *The Scarlet Letter, Moby Dick, The Marble Faun, Pierre,* and *Walden* were not nearly so widely read as books like Mrs. Kirkland's miscellanies. She also compiled during these decades several books of sentimental verse, wrote essays for anthologies of Americana, contributed still to magazines, and wrote a popular biography of Washington.

I *The Gift Books*

The Evening Book or, Fireside Talk on Morals and Manners, with Sketches of Western Life (1852) was the first collection—compiled not only for women her own age but for "youthful readers" who might be reading Mrs. Kirkland for the first time. Though she did not wish to be "frightfully serious" in the essays, as she stated in the preface, she did want to make it very clear that the purpose of the collections was a sober one: (1) to make a peculiarly American book "because the foreign literature which furnish[ed] most of the reading of our young people, seem[ed] . . . likely to inspire them with un-American ideas of society and even of duty" and (2) to reprint those essays and

sentimental tales whose "messages" spoke the "ancient and universal standards . . . the principles that govern the universal
human heart." [1] She did not want "to be set down as a mere
moralizer—a tiresome companion," [2] but she often became one.

The titles of some of the essays in *The Evening Book* suggested
the content: "The Household," a homily on the virtues associated
with the home; "A Chapter on Hospitality," "Conversation," and
"The Mystery of Visiting", essays on the social proprieties; "The
Significance of Dress" and "Fastidiousness," essays on the "fashionable" social sins. The brief tales—"exemplars," Mrs. Kirkland
called them—invoked the homely virtues of constancy, love,
friendship, and honor; and all were nicely etched with humor and
religious sentiment, capturing precisely the tone her women readers delighted in. Half of the collection was devoted to such topics
or to sentimental tales; the other half of the collection was given
over to Western sketches—that part which indeed made the
book "peculiarly American."

All but one of these sketches had been printed in the *Union;*
this one, "The Town Poor: A Western Reminiscence," had appeared first in *Arthur's Ladies' Magazine*.[3] It was a humorous account of a town's concern for a woman recently widowed, too
destitute—so she spread the rumor—to return to "York State," apparently to settle once again in her old home. The townsfolk col-
lected enough money for her to make the trip, which she took,
and then were amazed when she returned after the visit, as it had
been her intent all along. "The widow herself is meanwhile the
most unconcerned person in town. She declares that she had a
delightful visit, and wouldn't have missed it for anything," wrote
Mrs. Kirkland. "The 'charitable,' who contributed so readily . . .
feel a little sore; but all join in the laugh at the widow's triumph,
and agree to hold themselves outwitted." [4]

"Standards," an essay apparently written specifically for *The
Evening Book*, carried the conviction of Emerson's "Self-Reliance." Mrs. Kirkland declared that Americans did not need standards set by society and friends nearly so much as they needed
some individual standards: "a little more self-reliance, self-
recollection, self-respect . . . a more distinct perception of our
true interest and dignity . . . a clear-sighted preference of reality
to mere appearance of the inward to the outward." [5] Like Emerson and Thoreau, Mrs. Kirkland seemingly decried the American

practice that encouraged man's material well-being above his spiritual growth. The essay reflected the same disenchantment she
and her husband had experienced before they returned to the
East. The "inner man" was sacrificed to society's demand upon the
productive efforts of the "outer man."

*A Book for the Home Circle; or, Familiar Thoughts on Various
Topics, Literary, Moral and Social* (1853)—announced as "a
companion for *The Evening Book*—was the second collection,
more particularly addressed to the "youthful readers." She was
teaching school again, and with her pupils in mind she selected
the essays and tales which "record[ed] . . . observations and
conclusions on the subject of life and character." She hoped, she
continued in the preface, to find her "docile and gentle listeners"
receptive to her essays, to "accept kindly what is well intended." [6]
The "literary" essays were on novel reading (she recommended
novels of social purpose); authors (she was surprisingly critical of
women novelists); "lion-hunting" and autograph-seeking; literary women (they often forgot that their "greatest duty" was to be
women first, writers second); and lending books. The "moral"
pieces were the sentimental tales and the Western sketches, and
the "social" essays were on such subjects as neatness, giving and
receiving presents, and patience.

The Western sketches repeated regional material already
worked with. Mrs. Plummer in "Fashionable and Unfashionable"
regarded cleanliness as "almost the only beauty." She was an "in-
cessant scrubber, and left neither paint nor varnish on anything.
. . . Even the books, of which there was a shelf full in the par-
lour, were always wiped with a wet cloth when the room was
cleaned, for the good woman said she did not see why a book
must be left dirty any more than anything else." [7] Mother Plummer reminded the reader of Mrs. Doubleday in *A New Home,*
also a "scrubber." "Recollections of Rural Life in the West"—recollections reminiscent of characters and incidents in *A New
Home,* in *Forest Life* and in the *Union* articles—touched upon
such subjects as the needless destruction of the wilderness, the
problems of getting "hired girls," the miscarriages of frontier justice, the "steps to ruin" (drinking, gambling).

The lead essay in the collection, "Reading for Amusement,"
contained opinions already expressed in her articles, as well as in
her husband's, on the advantages of magazine writing. Part of the

essay is interesting to the modern reader because of her estimates of the American literary scene. Arguing again the position that the content of the British monthlies too often discouraged "in our young people due respect and affection for their native land," Mrs. Kirkland defended American magazines because of the moral tone in much of the fiction and verse. Admitting that American magazine writing was sometimes "jejune and frothy," she countered with what she regarded as particular strengths: (1) the "choicest fugitive poetry" of people like Bryant, Fitz-Greene Halleck, Longfellow, Willis, and Lowell; (2) the "elegant and instructive writers" like Miss Sedgwick, Mrs. Child, Poe, and Hoffman. And she correctly estimated the chief reason why American monthlies were not better: "proprietors of the magazines, who, holding the purse-strings, short-sightedly refuse to pay for any but 'amusing' articles, and look upon what is technically termed 'heavy matter,' as unsaleable. 'A thing must be *piquant*, or exciting,' say they, 'in order to go down'; and a 'piquant' treatise on natural philosophy, or an 'exciting' essay on some great principle in morals or political economy not being easily found, novelettes and sentimental poetry [too often] fill the whole field of interest." [8] The implications of her statements suggested both apology and explanation for her own shortcomings as editor of the *Union*.

Autumn Hours, and Fireside Reading (1854), the third collection, was once again written for her younger readers—understandably, it was the least satisfying collection since the better essays and tales had now been winnowed out. The bulk of the collection was a long story, "Search after Pleasure," which had served as the commentary in *The Book of Home Beauty* (1852). It was a framework story: a circle of friends, seeking an isolated "nook" for a summer holiday, passed their time profitably by composing chapters to a novel about the trials and tribulations of marriage, a coquette to a sober, maturer gentleman. The moral was obvious: the course of love never runs smoothly and pride and prejudice eventually dissolve with the power of love. The story carried matronly advice for the young women whom the author was addressing.

Among the shorter essays, "Women of the Revolution" gave brief accounts of heroic women in the North and the South with excerpts from their letters and journals to illustrate their courage and sacrifice. "Saints of Our Day" was in praise of benevolent men, particularly Father Isaac T. Hopper, a Quaker, who was instrumental in prison reform in New York. "Western Traits" was a regional essay on the warmth of Western hospitality. One story, "A Legend of East Rock," reminded the reader of the Indian-hater whom Hall wrote about in several Western sketches. Mrs. Kirkland's Indian-hater, however, had such remorse for his killing that he became a hermit, living on a desolate rock overlooking the village of New Haven, Connecticut.

II *Literary Miscellany—Books Edited or Written*

Although the Indian did not figure significantly in Mrs. Kirkland's sketches of Western life, she apparently had great sympathy for him. Such sympathy showed in the "legend" she retold and in the preface she supplied for Mrs. Mary Eastman's *Dahcotah; or, Life and Legends of the Sioux around Fort Snelling* (1849). Regarding the Indian essentially as a noble primitive— "the study of the Indian character is the study of the unregenerate [naive] human heart"—she shared with Mrs. Eastman the conviction that it was the white man's solemn Christian duty to improve "the wretched condition"—physical and spiritual—of the native American.

Mindful of the value of "authentic pictures of Indian life . . . [from] a literary point of view," she spoke of "the distinct and characteristic poetic material" a study of the Indian offered American authors in search of native themes. With a sentiment recalling Irving and Simms, she pointed out that the "shadowy" lives and "picturesque" traditions afforded writers a body of native lore—a heritage—uniquely theirs to explore in fiction and verse.

> It is said that our imitativeness is so servile, that for the sake of following English models, at an immeasurable distance, we neglect the new and grand material which lies all around us, in the sublime features of our country, in our new and striking circumstances, in our peculiar history and splendid prospects, and, above all, in the character, superstitions, and legends of our aborigines. . . . we are allowing these people, with so much of the heroic element in their lives, and so much of the mysterious in their origin, to go into the annihilation which seems their inevitable fate as civilization advances, without an effort to secure

and record all that they are able to communicate respecting themselves.

Observing that a humanitarian treatment of the Indian was in conflict with the "hurry of utilitarian progress" in America, she criticized her countrymen for their injustices:

> We . . . [look] upon [the Indian] as a thriftless, treacherous, drunken fellow, who knows just enough to be troublesome, or who must be cajoled or forced into leaving his hunting-grounds for the occupation of very orderly and virtuous white people, who sell him gunpowder and whiskey, but send him now and then a missionary to teach him that it is wrong to get drunk and murder his neighbor. To look upon the Indian with much regard, even in the light of literary material, would be inconvenient; for the moment we recognize in him a mind, a heart, a soul,—the recollection of the position in which we stand towards him becomes thorny, and we begin dimly to remember certain duties belonging to our Christian profession, which we have sadly neglected with regard to the sons of the forest, whom we have driven before us just as fast as we have required or desired their lands.

These sentiments, of course, were not original—not even distinctive; but they reinforced a view shared by many of her literary contemporaries. Only Cooper and Miss Sedgwick had, in Mrs. Kirkland's opinion, attempted an honest appraisal of the Indian in their work by using him as native material, by pointing out the white man's errors, and by "making him the poetical machine in fiction." She praised Mrs. Eastman's book moderately: "in its character of aesthetic material for another age, it appeals to our nationality." [9] There was in Mrs. Eastman's book only a pale realistic hue, for a thick romantic haze colored the record "taken down from the very lips of the red people"—so thick, in fact, Mrs. Kirkland was restricted to writing largely pleasantries. Realistic sketches of life in the West, they were not; but the opportunity to write the preface came at a time when Mrs. Kirkland needed quick cash.

Another piece of work was a preface supplied for Mrs. Marian Reid's *Woman, Her Education and Influence* (1848). Mrs. Reid was a militant feminist; and speculation leads one to consider how much more liberal Mrs. Kirkland would have been in her thinking had circumstances in her life been different, had William Kirkland lived, had she not been forced to compete as a nineteenth-century American woman in a man's world. Although Mrs. Kirkland seemed to believe that "woman's vocation [was] to persuade, not to command," she was obviously annoyed with "woman's sphere" as it was circumscribed in mid-century America. She did not endorse suffrage and party politics for women, as Mrs. Reid did; but she did demand equal economic status, greater civil rights in courts of law, an expanded system of public education, and opportunity for frank expression of opinion. She acknowledged women's social influence but accused them of "slavish timidity" when it came to claiming their rights. Asserting a sentiment which was often a persistent one in many of the essays and tales printed in the gift annuals, she declared that "the principles of Christianity must finally overcome every thing else in the conduct of this world's affairs. . . . When the first question asked in State affairs shall be, 'What is right?' instead of the more usual one, 'What is expedient for present interest?' [then] the voice of woman will be heard, for good and not for evil." [10] The preface began with an unfortunate analogy;[11] but the strength of conviction led to an energetic, forceful statement of principles—one, on occasion, unhesitatingly blunt. Not since *A New Home* had she been as forthright with her readers: anger, injustice, and doubtless personal experience prompted the outburst of resentment.

For quick money, too, she had prepared a book, *Spenser and the Faery Queen* (1847), in spite of the note in the preface that the book was "actuated solely by a desire to see Spenser more read in this country." [12] The excerpts from the *Faerie Queene* were taken from Book One—"the cream of the work"; a biographical essay and a cursory analysis of the poem with brief comment about the allegory—"too subtle and obscure to be made intelligible to the general reader" without some explanation—were hastily concocted for the text. Two essays also appeared in collections of Americana: one article on Bryant for *Homes of American Authors* (1853) and one on Washington for *Homes of American Statesmen* (1854). The article on Bryant is interesting because of their friendship. "Few people," Keyes observed, "had known Bryant so well as Mrs. Kirkland. His home and home life were almost as familiar to her as her own." [13]

The article on Washington no doubt prompted her book on the

national hero, but there is little in her hortatory biography of
Washington to commend it to the modern reader. She had read
Mason Locke Weems's biography and Jared Sparks's life history
and the first volumes of Irving's biography; her book—the *Per-
sonal Memoirs of George Washington* (1857)—complemented
Weems's anecdotal approach. She wrote a correspondent, possibly
Sparks, her intent in the biography:

> I am writing a book about Washington—for the use of *young peo-
> ple.*— So far as I know there is none exactly suited to interest
> them—and I have so much to do with them, young ladies espe-
> cially,—that I fancy I can make a Life of Washington better
> calculated for them than any that I know of. . . . I spend my
> mornings at the Department of State, where is the invaluable
> box of M.S.S. purchased of the W—— heirs by the government,
> at the cost of $20,000— My design is to give a more private
> and *imitable* view of Washington than the great historians have
> done— It has been said, you know, that Washington "had no pri-
> vate character"— The Washington family tell a very different
> story—and so do the Washington M.S.S. Indeed I would fain
> seize the spirit of the truth, and tell the story as I conceive it.[14]

She intended her book for young people to be as "familiar and
home-like a life of the great man, as can be gathered from his own
papers and the sayings of his contemporaries." [15] It was an informal biography, sentimental, feminine in appeal, pietistic:

> From the earliest record we possess of the career of Washing-
> ton, we find the sense of duty always connected in his mind with
> the hope of success; the idea of cooperation with Divine Law
> with the dependence on Divine aid. He evidently felt that obedi-
> ence is strength. Nothing less than this could have supported
> him, under the public reproaches and private sneers that goaded
> him incessantly, during the earlier part of the war, when a single
> yielding up of duty to the selfish desire of personal reputation,
> might have covered him with glory and ruined our cause.
>
> This point—the dignity of ennobling uses of obedience, and the
> danger of its being almost forgotten in our American scheme of
> education—was too important to be passed lightly over, in an
> attempt to trace the early training of Washington, and to discover
> what were some of the accessories in the formation of a character
> so weighty and so benignant. Our readers must excuse this in-

stance of prolixity. It seemed desirable to connect the consideration of an unpopular virtue with the character of one, confessedly
the first of men, in whom it was so strikingly operative. Acknowl-
edging at the outset that we look upon Washington as the ideal
American man—not the slow and dogged Saxon, or the mercurial
and chivalric Norman, but a product of both, and different from
both—it follows that in making him a pattern, the American rises
toward a high point of virtue; in departing from such a model
he sinks to a lower grade. When we have seen an American of
nobler and more admirable character . . . we may, without loss,
set aside this one, vouchsafed us by Almighty Providence as a
birth-gift to our young republic, at once a pattern for its character
and a promise for its fortune. The self-control, the economy, the
courage, the enterprise, the public spirit, the religiousness, which
distinguished Washington, are the component points of the true
American character, which has little ancestral *prestige* or inspiration to rely on, which has no "privilege" to shield corruption,
no "caste" to dignify vice. Our wealth is suddenly acquired,
bringing of course great necessity for self-control; it is continually
changing hands, making economical habits peculiarly necessary.
Our vast resources originating vast designs, enterprise becomes
a splendid quality; the facility occasioned by a division of responsibility, is too often the source of official corruption; true public spirit—the vital spark of national self-government—is the most
difficult of virtues. Self-assertion and worldliness being our ever-
present snare, amid such unexampled opportunities of material
prosperity, religion is our best safeguard and highest wisdom—the
only citadel of our liberties, the only voucher for their perpetuity.
When we remember these things, let us remember also, that
Washington was the model in all of them; and, wisely looking
back to first causes in so important a matter, let us not disdain to
lay foundations of character, upon which it shall at least be possible for so high and noble a structure to stand.

God pardon us for ever holding lightly so great a blessing as
this model; for praising Washington in words . . . we persuade
ourselves, is an advance in the spirit of the age.

Circumstances and customs change, but the standard of character is eternal.[16]

Mrs. Kirkland objected to reading Washington's letters: "an old-
fashioned directness; often a disposition to moralize, and always a
serious tone." [17] A similar comment might well define the reader's
objection to her book.[18]

For young readers, too, she compiled *Garden Walks with the*

Poets (1852) and *The School-Girl's Garland* (1864)—predominantly collections of verse from American poets. But her *Holidays Abroad; or Europe from the West* (1849) was simply another travel account. The Duyckincks' disappointment in the book might reflect the reader's:

> We could wish that Mrs. Kirkland . . . had given us more of the west by introducing some of the characters of her "New Home," or "Forest Life," into the heart of Europe, and setting forth their adventures in the dramatic form of Smollett's Humphrey Clinker. . . . As it is, we are not often reminded of any . . . peculiarities which once belonged to the "West," unless we set down an occasional independence of guide books and stereotyped opinion, with an intolerable aversion to the tyranny of that despotic gentleman, the courier, to this account. The most genuine pieces of Westernisms which we have noticed, are a translation of . . . *gateau aux fraises* into strawberry short-cake, and the cool mention of the sick lady smitten with a fever at Rome— "As I understood, she stops at Passignano to take her shake." [19]

The West, which had made "an indelible impression" on her mind —so she declared in the preface to *A Book for the Home Circle*— and which as a place of great interest to her was "undiminished," [20] was, however, no longer an experience in her life. The Western influence that gave *A New Home* and *Forest Life* and some of the Western sketches so much spirit—so much freshness and exuberance, so much wit and sprightly narration, so much charm and delight—had been extinguished in the course of living in the East. The "bead [was] gone forever"; it had dried up in the passage of time.

III   *Comments on Writing*

Mrs. Kirkland never worked out a literary theory, but what she had to say about writing and writers can be found in the articles she prepared for the magazines and in the essays she culled for the gift books.[21] To begin, she was professedly American in her viewpoint: good writing reflected the nation's history and its ideals: "if a writer will only tell very long stories about the 'Revolution war,' or very tough ones about the Indians," she declared in *Forest Life*, "and if the said stories be very bloody and very marvellous, we will believe every word, and, believing, enjoy." [22]

In a brief book review in the *Union,* in praise of Irving and Bryant, she elaborated: "The works that have . . . given the most pleasure [to] all [Americans], have been those which refer to our early history, the sacrifices and triumphs of our fathers, the gradual improvement of society among us, the researches into the first settlement[s] of our continent. . . ." [23] One of the duties of the writer, then, was to suggest an essence of the national image in the stories he wrote. Her view paralleled in part that of writers of American historical romance in that readers learned something about Americans of a former age: they learned something of the character and spirit, the achievements, and the ambitions of their forefathers. Such knowledge brought respect. And the writer who conceived of writing in such a way contributed greatly toward the development of a national literature. Writing which depicted the American character and American life—past or present—was for Mrs. Kirkland an appropriate claim for serious consideration by readers.

Her interest in social history, as *A New Home* and as *Forest Life* had made abundantly clear, led to an appreciation of novels whose object it was to present "our tangled and confused social web"—that is, novels of social purpose. [24] Yet she strongly objected to the early French realists, such as Balzac and George Sand, who exhibited in their books social problems better left undiscussed. Mrs. Kirkland was sufficiently a woman of her age to believe that some truth was not worth telling, that some truth indeed could not be properly told, and that each writer had to decide where to draw the line. She wrote several essays criticizing the works of George Sand, whom she disliked intensely not only for her unwomanly behavior but also for her bad taste in writing about certain social conditions. "George Sand," she flatly asserted, "is the unsuspected flatterer of all who are discontented with their own lot, and who find gratification in shifting the responsibility from themselves to society and its institutions and abuses." [25] Mrs. Kirkland contended that society was not at fault so much as individuals themselves who were anxious to make society a scapegoat for their own failures and predilections.

Indeed, she was quite suspicious of that "dim horror" on the literary scene—the literary woman. [26] Yet such "horrors" were in the minority, she believed; and men whose business it was to lead and instruct ought not really to fear "usurpation." Women should be women first; writers or professional persons, second. "One great duty of wom[e]n, if not the greatest, is to be agreeable . . . ," she advised her readers. "The natural desire to be agreeable . . . [is] quite strong enough. . . ." [27] To stand well with men outweighed the momentary success literary efforts might bring.

She stressed the efficacy of magazine writing which did much "to elevate the intellectual and moral character of the people"; she believed that magazines "constitute[d] in a country like ours, a powerful element of civilization." [28] She had some reservations about indiscriminate novel reading, an echo of an earlier age. In one essay she wrote, she told the story of a young woman whose "knowledge" of the world came through novel reading and who used this "knowledge" to find herself a husband. It was a false knowledge, Mrs. Kirkland pointed out; she cautioned her readers against "those instructive and veracious histories of the world and its doings, called novels." [29] One of the real dangers of random novel reading, particularly novels by European authors, was that they encouraged "a certain knowingness which . . . can hardly be considered as exerting a healthful influence on American minds. Their morality is often scarcely strict enough for our Puritan notions," she warned. Additionally, "their flings at the political maxims which we, as Americans, are bound to hold most sacred, are far from encouraging in our young people due respect and affection for their native land." [30]

Much of her own work in the magazines after her return from the West was written for women and young people. The preface to *The Evening Book* announced that this collection of her writing was principally concerned with essays on the values and virtues of American life: "it becomes," she wrote, "especially desirable to refer sometimes to the ancient and universal standards—those whose excellence is beyond dispute." [31] She would risk "growing intolerably serious" to impress upon her readers the wisdom of homely American virtues.[32] "If they [the readers] should feel a tap now and then, we must say to them as the conscientious Quaker did to his wife when he was administering domestic discipline,— 'Why does thee cry so? It's all for thy own good!' " [33]

Like Irving, she lamented the eroding away of home-bred virtues and believed that loss of them in the home was one of the reasons for the "general decay" in society. "If love and truth, justice and religion, reigned in our homes, so would they in social life," she reminded her readers; "if pride, desire of display, and of appearing what we are not; if a longing for excitement; a secret indulgence of vicious inclinations . . . characterize our household life, so will they [infect] . . . 'Society' which we are fond of making a scape-goat of. The decay of the household fire is the cause of our social coldness; if we would have our outer intercourse rational, unaffected, sympathetic, improving, and beneficent, we must reform [our] domestic maxims." [34] She emphasized more than once in her essays what she believed to be a large reason for the "decay" in American society: the slavish and foolish imitation of customs and manners of European society—a society really alien to American culture.

Mrs. Kirkland was always the moralist in her essays, and she looked for a moral principle in all she read and in all she praised. Books, like good conversation among friends, were "moral engine[s]." [35] One ought not worry if a book he lent was not returned, she said once: "you have at least done your utmost toward the dissemination of the good it contain[ed]. . . ." [36] " 'A wholesome tongue *is* a tree of life!' " she quoted Proverbs. In their literature Americans stood for morality, delicacy, decency. There was a line beyond which the moralist would not go in his quest for material. Propriety was always the governing alembic.

She was not nearly so interested in form and expression as she was in sentiment. The significant thing was the message the writing contained. "The first demand . . . is that a writer shall say something," Mrs. Kirkland observed, "and only . . . second that he shall say it well. Mere style is but little esteemed, except so far as it has direct fitness to convey ideas clearly." And she advised her readers, in forming their own judgment of the worth of a piece of writing, that "not only good common sense, but taste, knowledge, sensibility, and sympathy are required to make literary judgment worth anything. . . . We must know," she concluded, "what a work ought to be, before we are competent to say what it is." [37]

Mrs. Kirkland was not a judicious critic, but she was perhaps a sensible one for the position she held. She emphasized Americanism, appreciation of the home-bred virtues, morality in fiction, moderation, decency, and respect. Although she had said some years before that "nine tenths of the magazine stories . . . have nothing to do with this life" and that "fiction which has no relation to what has been, or what is to be . . . [is] both vapid and value-less," she apparently forgave writers of such stories if they offered "instruction" to readers. Indeed, instruction was the prime requisite of good writing—a requisite her Western material and her essays and sentimental pieces in the magazines provided. From such instruction, she felt, American readers would benefit and the moral progress of American society would be assured.

IV *Shorter Essays and Fiction*

There is something left to say about Mrs. Kirkland's fugitive articles—essays and sentimental tales—that appeared in magazines like the *Columbian, Knickerbocker's, Godey's, Peterson's,* the *Broadway Journal,* and *Putnam's* during the 1840's and 1850's. "Vincent Hervey, or the Man of Impulse" related the story of a naïve young man who made all the wrong choices. A sentimental tale with the inevitable moral, it is not unlike Melville's *Pierre* in theme, where "right intentions" cause nearly disastrous consequences.[38]

"The Belles of Etherington" approached in structure a short story, one of the very few pieces of fiction Mrs. Kirkland wrote which deserves the title. It was the story of two young women, orphaned Fanny Aston and her cousin Cornelia Beverley, who loved the same young man, Fred Leaming. He in turn had a rival in Edward Beverley for the affections of Fanny. The brother and sister plotted revenge for their wounded pride; and Fred, after a streak of bad luck, took to running illegal contraband to get quick money to marry Fanny and remove her from her cousins' influence. He was apprehended and killed by Edward, who drowned in the icy river trying to recover the contraband. After the "dreadful catastrophe" and the "bitterness of grief," the two young women were reconciled and joined together "in alleviating the woes of others." The four characters were well developed, and the plot was economically manipulated to the climax when the tragedy occurred. The stoic reserve of the women, determined to lead useful lives, recalls Sarah Orne Jewett's Maine women.[39]

It is impossible to identify positively the articles Mrs. Kirkland wrote for the *Broadway Journal* and *Putnam's.* There are, of course, Poe's statements and Briggs's that she was a contributor to their journals.[40] Only one notice appears in the *Broadway Journal* under her name—a notice soliciting money and furnishings for a

home to be established in New York for discharged women convicts;[41] yet a number of articles in the *Broadway Journal* are unsigned, and such sentimental tales as those sketches under the
general title "The Devices of Beggary" and essays on city amusements, reform, and writing for magazines, as well as book reviews
and notices of concerts, art exhibitions, and the theater, may have
come from her pen.[42] It was contrary to Briggs's policy in *Putnam's*
to have articles signed by contributors, although pseudonyms
sometimes appeared;[43] yet once again essays on such topics as
New York charities, education, American manners, the early years
of Washington, public amusements, as well as book reviews, may
be Mrs. Kirkland's material.[44] Along with Mrs. Kirkland's unsigned
essays in the pages of *Putnam's*, there are, of course, unsigned
stories like "Bartleby, the Scrivener" and "The Lightning-Rod
Man" and the novel *Israel Potter*. And Salvator R. Tarnmoor is
identified as the author of "The Encantadas, or Enchanted Isles."

Mrs. Kirkland was not upset by anonymity; she preferred it.
In a letter to Francis Bowen of the *North American,* she once
asked, "Can't I be 'Mrs A'—meaning Mrs Anonymous?" The publication of her name, she felt, hampered her.

> I lack courage to give opinions, especially when they happen
> not to chime in with the received ones—when I am to be held
> personally answerable, as I do not choose to defend myself. I
> have been scolded not a little for some trifles in my notice[s] . . .
> and I do not like it. Indeed as a general rule I think the blazon-
> ing of the names of writers hurts the freedom and the influence
> of reviewers— They [the reviews] ought to stand on their own
> merits and not on the reputation or no-reputation of their authors,
> who can hardly be expected to enjoy the full use of their faculties
> with a sword hanging over their heads which is quite as likely to
> fall for some trivial inadvertence as for an essential matter. At
> any rate I think ladies should be excused.[45]

Although she wrote a number of patriotic articles during the
Civil War, she devoted most of her energies to more immediate
war work. One of her essays was a review of the war effort in
Illinois, which she had observed when she visited her son Joseph
who was now living there. Joseph Kirkland, in fact, published
posthumously three of his mother's short pieces in the short-lived
Prairie Chicken.[46] The point of view expressed in one of these

pieces, "Town or Country?," confirmed emphatically Mrs. Kirkland's long absence from the West:

> . . . a city home can have few things said against it, and the city offers so many social advantages that one must be stupid indeed to undervalue a residence in it. If the country gives us Nature, the city gives Art; if the country abounds in liberty, the city abounds equally in resources. If in the country we have leisure, in the city we find society at will. Country lanes are pleasant in good weather; city pavements are very convenient in bad. Green trees wave in the breeze to gladden our ruralized eyes; white sails gleam in the blue waters that surround us in town—*our* town of New York. . . .[47]

She might have been vexed at times with "the state of the frog market" in New York;[48] she might have found *her* city indifferent at times and lonely for a widow with children to support; she might have been angered by the restrictions placed upon her because she was only a woman in a man's world; yet the conviction she expressed in *Forest Life* twenty years before was undiminished. The "inner man" was nourished in the city, nowhere else. There were evenings with "pleasant talkers"[49]—with "Mr. Poe and any other gentleman or gentle*men* likely to be agreeable";[50] and with Mrs. Botta, Miss Sedgwick, Mrs. Child, and other New York literati. There was the satisfaction of molding young minds in the schools where she taught.[51] There was simply the "magnificent city; a city of unexampled growth and energy; of the noblest public works . . . and of growing interest in all the arts which adorn and harmonize society."[52]

The writing she did do in the time she had free from her duties with the Sanitary Commission was frequently for *The Continental Monthly Magazine*, which published "war literature" for "loyal men and women . . . and all [the] soldiers."[53] She solicited her old literary friends for contributions; and in a note to Halleck in February, 1864, thanking him for a poem, she reminisced about an earlier time: "The book I am reading now is Irving's life—and it makes me almost young again. The days when we were looking for new works from him and from the author of 'Fanny,' etc were my palmy days!"[54]

Mrs. Kirkland had been indeed fortunate in her chosen profession. The reading public had been kind to her and to so many of her literary friends; she had had a good life—writing, teaching, and performing public services. When she died suddenly two months later, she was deeply and happily engaged in editing a volume of poetry for her young friends and in managing an exhibition for the Sanitary Commission Fair.

CHAPTER 6

"Valuable Only for Its Truth":
An Appraisal

. . . My life has been one of much sorrow and it would be painful to me to have it dragged before the public. I would rather be known by my writings only—except to my friends—who can do as they like after my death— If I knew which of my writings are most characteristic, I would make the selection—but I do not— I have thought some of my articles from the Union were as good as any I ever wrote.

—Mrs. Kirkland to John S. Hart [1]

. . . The reader who has the patience to go with me to the close of my desultory sketches, must expect nothing beyond a meandering recital of common-place occurrences—mere gossip about everyday people, little enhanced in value by any fancy or ingenuity of the writer; in short, a very ordinary pen-drawing; which, deriving no interest from coloring, can be valuable only for its truth.

—*A New Home*

M RS. CAROLINE M. KIRKLAND was a sensitive woman who was reluctant to bring attention to herself personally and who was happier to direct readers' curiosity toward her writing. Her mature estimate of her work, and her wish always for anonymity after her return to New York, bore out her belief that the essay itself—not the personality that wrote it—was more important for the purposes she had in mind. The regional sketches were apparently less significant to her than the material primarily written for magazines and gift books. The modern reader discounts Mrs. Kirkland's estimate of her own work, although her opinion did coincide with that of editors and anthologists of American literature in the 1850's.

Griswold and the Duyckincks among others, remembering only briefly that she was the author of *A New Home*, too often praised her less original work. Hart in *Female Prose Writers of America* professed "no hesitation in saying, that of all [the *Union's*] brilliant array of contributors, there was not one whose articles gave such entire and uniform satisfaction as those of Mrs. Kirkland. . . . [her] essays . . . form . . . her strongest claim to distinction as a writer." [2] Hart and Mrs. Kirkland, discrediting the early regional sketches, were too much aware of the feminine 1850's in which they were both writing—aware of the popular tastes, aware of the role they felt fiction and the essay played in the conduct of their readers' lives. Literary exercises which dealt in ennobling sentiments and public morality, and which praised American life and manners—not sketches of Western backwoods eccentricities and vulgar beliefs—were "claim[s] to distinction." Melville earned only abuse and oblivion when he chose to ignore the readers' tastes. The modern reader, however, unwilling to accept this view of Mrs. Kirkland's talent, wishes she might have realized—as he does with the advantage of literary history and the perspective of American writers' accomplishments—that her lasting contribution was the different view of life she introduced in the Western sketches: realism.

It was doubtless the reception of the Western sketches in Michigan that led her to disavow the good work she had done. Hurt by the outbursts of friends and neighbors when they read *A New Home* and remorseful over the imagined wrongs, she tried to make amends in *Forest Life*: "ingenious malice has been busy in finding substance for the shadows which were called up to give variety to the pages of 'A New Home,'" she wrote in the preface; "I have been accused of substituting personality for impersonation . . . and I am sincerely sorry that any one has been persuaded to regard as unkind what was announced merely as a playful sketch, and not as a serious history." The "playful sketches" in *A New Home* and in *Forest Life* were missing in *Western Clearings*. Humor which gave life and warmth to Westerners in Montacute and along the Michigan frontier was replaced by sullen anger in the miscellany—a series of distorted incidents of Western life in a despoiled Eden. Thereafter, she wrote only "shadows"—essays and sketches on general topics of general interest—and eschewed all comment on men and their eccentricities. She retreated to safer material—less personal and less censurable for the readers of her day but more open to criticism by readers today.

The essays and sentimental tales—unlike the Western material —were noncontroversial, and she found editors willing to accept them for the pages of women's magazines. These stories and essays pleased everyone: no one was offended by the fictitious representations or by the heavy sentiment. And in the years of sorrow and some apparent privation following her husband's death, Mrs. Kirkland wrote the kind of stuff that gave her quick money and easy access to the magazines and a reading public in the East with whom she had no quarrel.

Hers was not an enviable life: meeting deadlines, seeking contributors, writing correspondents, and finding time to set down her own random thoughts and observations. The routine described by Mrs. Mary G. Clarke, editor of *Mother's Journal,* was surely Mrs. Kirkland's for many years:

> First, in the morning read six pages of proof . . . and wrote a note to the printer. Superintended baking of pies and bread, and received a morning call from a friend. Adjusted two sleeping apartments, and prepared the children for school. Wrote a circular for the next volume of the [magazine]. Assisted in putting a spread on the frame, and marking it for quilting. Examined several business letters, and sent off numbers [of the magazine], ordered by new subscribers, to Post Office. Wrote a second note to the printer. Ironed a dress. Wrote two long letters to agents. Finished off a garment, previously commenced for one of the children. Looked over, and put to the proper places, the family washing. . . . [Answered] to the oft-repeated, "Mother!" which came from the lips of three children . . . besides the little wifely duties which came in to fill spaces; the contrivings of "what is for tea and for breakfast, ma'am," and the shadows of inquiries about to-morrow's dinner, which is to be shared with guests.[3]

Although Mrs. Clarke commands a sense of humor, Mrs. Kirkland more often than not forgets hers—in print, at least; for much of her magazine material is sober in view and in content. Her spontaneity is gone; impressions no longer personal are no longer fresh and vivid. As arbiter of the public taste, she took her new responsibility earnestly.[4] Taken as a whole, the material may have little appeal for the modern reader to whom it seems artificial in style, mannered in phrasing, unoriginal in thought—merely echoing sentiments and opinions already well-known and acceptable to women readers. But the modern reader must remember that Mrs. Kirkland, in choosing a career as a popular journalist, wrote successfully for a number of years the kind of magazine material most in demand by editors and readers; and she bent all her efforts toward distinction within this somewhat limited sphere. In this light, her essays are not only representative but often far better in style, quality, and content than those of many contributors to the magazines.[5]

However, when Poe praised her so warmly in "The Literati of New York City," he was speaking of the Mrs. Kirkland he had recently met—Mrs. Mary Clavers lately returned from the American West.

As Mrs. Mary Clavers, a spirited and perceptive critic of the Middle West, she played a distinctive role in American social history and in the development of American regional writing. Bayard Taylor, commenting in the New York *Tribune*, summarized a common editorial opinion: "She has represented a particular period in our social existence with so much success that her works, though slight in their fabric, and familiar in their tone, are likely to have a permanent existence and enforce a permanent interest. She is only a sketcher, but with so clear an eye and vigorous a touch as to afford just views of the present and valuable suggestions for the future." [6] As a social critic, often as a social satirist, and as an early regionalist, she is as rewarding a writer to the modern reader as she was to her earlier contemporaries—a commentator much more like Miss Austen than her professed model Miss Mitford.

As a pioneer in realistic studies, she contributed significantly to the American literary tradition. In *A New Home* and in *Forest Life*, she was the careful realist, faithful to the scenes she described. In spite of her neighbors' charges, her humor, sympathy, and understanding did not allow her to forget a sense of perspective, to lose hold of the chain of humanity. In her analysis of character, she was candid; but she did not exaggerate. "A portrait, however showily painted, is worth nothing, if it be not a resemblance," she wrote in *Forest Life*. "A painter would show his skill but poorly, who, in his zeal for beautifying his subject, should leave out a wart, even though it grew on the tip of one's nose. Equally unwise is he who exaggerates a wrinkle, or throws too heavy a shade over a complexion that needs no deepening." [7]

As an interpreter of the frontier, particularly in *Forest Life,* she was fortunate in that she was compelled to submit to the hardships; but she was determined not to yield to its narrowing, monotonous society. As Mrs. Knudsen has pointed out, the rough impact of the unromantic wilderness on an intelligent, sensitive woman from the East stimulated her more intensely than any other experience she was ever to have. The disappointment to the modern reader is that she spent the rest of her literary life denying it. Yet she saw the frontier with a clarity as no writer before her had pictured it. Her closest rival, James Hall, saw it through a romantic vision, as more than one reviewer noted. "For the West, Mary Claver [*sic*], the most agreeable and original of American female writers . . . is one of the best writers of western sketches and manners we have seen," wrote one critic; "she pursues a course, and occupies a prominence in historic authorship [as a chronicler of manners], quite distinct from Judge Hall. The latter writer illustrates rather the historical romance of the west . . . than the manner of the present race of emigrants. . . . Her sprightliness, good sense, high feeling, keen penetration, are inexhaustible." [8]

Even of greater interest to the modern reader is the fact that she is a forerunner of the darker realists who were to write about life in America—frequently, about life in the Middle West—in the years after the Civil War: men like Garland and Howe and her own son, Joseph Kirkland.

Certainly the distinguishing features of Western life she identified in her books were the ones these men explored in their regional fiction. Hamlin Garland's stories of the Middle Border emphasized a life of crushing toil and showed men and women heavily burdened by the dreary routine of farm life. It was an oppressive life—as Mrs. Kirkland had indicated—without grace, beauty, or homely charm: a treadmill on which embittered men got nowhere. Garland wrote about the forces which shaped the farmers' lives in *Main-Travelled Roads* (1891): futile anger at their lot in life, as Grant McLane showed in "Up the Coulé"; stubbornness to win out against odds—man-made or natural—at the cost of exhausted body and spirit, as Tim Haskins proved in

"Under the Lion's Paw"; restlessness which urged men to look elsewhere for the promised El Dorado, as Rob Rodemaker had done in "Among the Corn-Rows." "Local color," Garland said later in *Crumbling Idols* (1894), "means that it has such quality and texture and background that it could not have been written in any other place. . . ." A sense of furious despair overwhelmed the characters in *Main-Travelled Roads,* a life denying men a feeling of accomplishment and their women of happiness. Pictures of such a life were described patiently in Mrs. Kirkland's Western sketches, which Garland might well have read on the advice of his close friend Joseph Kirkland.

Edgar Watson Howe in *The Story of a Country Town* (1883) angrily denied the idyllic portrait of frontier living which Irving, Hall, and the other romancers had popularized: it was not the good life, particularly in the villages. Like Mrs. Kirkland, he emphasized the niggardly existence in Western towns, where villagers resorted to gossip and petty squabbling to relieve the tedium. Like Mrs. Kirkland, he also emphasized the drabness of pioneer villages: trees were felled; houses were unpainted. Ned Westlock remembered only weather-beaten buildings set against an ugly, bleak landscape.

Of all the regionalists, Joseph Kirkland was obviously most profoundly impressed by his mother's sketches. He wrote in an autobiographical sketch some years after that in his fiction he wished to follow "the path marked out by his mother in her *New Home.*" [9] He could limn character as well as his mother, identifying that trait which motivated a person's life. Zury Prouder had the fierce independence and iron will of many Westerners, and he earned his reputation as "the meanest man" by doggedly subduing his finer nature and his more generous impulses to the demands of "business": to get what only money could buy on the frontier, a sense of security. Anne Sparrow, the schoolteacher from the East, had a gentler nature which also hardened in her resolute purpose to "accommodate," to adapt to the urgency of frontier living. John McVey, Anne's first husband, was lazy and shiftless—an idler who let his wife do the farm work; he escaped to California where he died of fever. These characters were drawn from frontier types whom Kirkland had known and read about in his mother's books.

In *Zury: The Meanest Man in Spring County* (1887), men and women responded violently to the harsh struggle for existence

—farm work must be done, crops must be harvested; poverty always haunted the uneasy farmers. If lives became warped and twisted, it was the result of hard work and harrowing privation and singleness of purpose which the environment nurtured. Like his mother, Kirkland presented a picture of backwoods life stripped of romanticism and true in the details he chose to incorporate.

Garland complained that writers in America had too long imitated writing conventions and literary traditions of the past, had too often written not to please themselves but somebody else. They did not have the courage of their convictions and were blinded to the power of life around them. The task of the writer in America—he said in *Crumbling Idols*—was to create, not to imitate—"to produce [not] something *greater* than the past but . . . something *different* from the past." In denying the romantic tendency in much of the writing in her own day and in incorporating those distinguishing features of Western life which took the measure of frontier living, Mrs. Kirkland did "[produce] something *different* from the past"; and she pointed the way for these younger writers who created for the first time in American fiction life stripped of its glamor. They revealed its harshness and unloveliness, and they candidly said what Mrs. Kirkland had said: this is life in the Middle West. In the words of Joseph Kirkland, they told "the truth unadorned and unvarnished." [10]

It was, of course, the frontier environment that tied Mrs. Kirkland more closely to these regionalists than it did to other American writers of local manners—to men like George Washington Cable and Joel Chandler Harris and to women like Mary Noailles Murfree, Mary E. Wilkins Freeman, and Sarah Orne Jewett. These writers had a mellower view of man and nature which their experience and observation allowed. Their province was not the one carved out by Mrs. Kirkland.

For Garland, Howe, and Joseph Kirkland, however, who grew up in the Middle West, life was viewed darkly—bitterness, disappointments, and frustrations amounted in their fiction to the discouraging picture of life. They were not naturalists;[11] but their vision of life was dreary, routine, and restricting. The harshness of life produced ugliness: sometimes indifference, sometimes revolt, often self-centeredness. These aspects of frontier life Mrs. Kirkland reported clearly in the Western sketches. Dishonesty, bitterness, hunger, and privation more often than not permanently scarred the inhabitants of the West. Nature was relentless—as in "The Hard Winter"—and men aped nature's way. There were heroic figures like Sam Jennings, Richard Brand, Aunty Parshalls; but more often men like Silas Ashburn disintegrated under the hard struggle against the wilderness; and women like Mrs. Lowndes degenerated into slatterns, unkempt, shiftless, and shrewish. This coarsening life, this disillusioning vision, forced the Kirklands to the East again so that such dreams and hopes as parents have about their children and their future could have a better chance of being fulfilled.

A woman's sympathy went out to the poor and oppressed, and Mrs. Kirkland was not blind to the courage of many of her neighbors. It was the destitute families in the clearings whom she thought about when the wild-cat banks burst and the hoarded banknotes became valueless; it was the weary, distraught housewife numbly performing the work around the farm whom she remembered when she heard that the husband was near death, crushed by the tree he was felling. She was always aware of the ravages of the ague; she was humble when she had food to share with less fortunate neighbors. Yet she never forgot the ignorance, prejudice, and false pride some of her Montacute neighbors showed. This portion of her portrait of the West—the desolation of families and the shoddy republicanism practiced by many Westerners—makes her work memorable to the modern reader. When she saw the West clearly in *A New Home,* in *Forest Life,* in the best of the sketches, and in *Western Clearings,* she often saw it tragically.

Mrs. Kirkland is not an Irving who paints still-life primitives; she is not a Hall who seeks the romantic frontiersman; she is not a Hoffman who is vague but enthusiastic about a month's horseback tour through the backwoods. In her best work, Mrs. Kirkland implies what Alfred Kazin has called the tragic vision of American life—a vision that was to emerge steadily with her followers in the decades after the Civil War.

Notes and References

Chapter One

1. Typescript copy of letter dated Utica, December 25, 1826, to William Kirkland, in the Joseph Kirkland Papers, Newberry Library.

2. *Ibid.*

3. Letter from Samuel Stansbury to his mother, Sarah Ogier Stansbury, dated [New York], November 16, 1801. Quoted in Mrs. Louise N. Knudsen, "Caroline Kirkland, Pioneer"—unpublished master's thesis, Michigan State College of Agriculture and Applied Science, 1934.

4. "Is Patience a Virtue?—An Autobiography" in *A Book for the Home Circle* (published as "Conduct and Consequences: An Autobiography," *Graham's Magazine*, XXII [March, 1843], 150–57); and "An Incident in Dream-Land" in *Autumn Hours* (published under same title in *Graham's Magazine*, XXII [June, 1843], 335–36).

5. Moses Coit Tyler, *The Literary History of the American Revolution 1763–1783*, II (New York, 1957), 80.

6. Mr. Langley C. Keyes writes in his doctoral dissertation: "old encyclopedias in their accounts of Samuel Stansbury have pitched upon the unhappy episode of the stationery and book store as the principal occupation of his life. Obviously it was merely one of a number of unsuccessful ventures that mark his earlier years." "Caroline M. Kirkland: A Pioneer in American Realism," unpublished Ph.D. dissertation, Harvard University, 1935, p. 88. I am indebted to Mr. Keyes's admirable study for factual information regarding Mrs. Kirkland's formative years.

7. Keyes, p. 91.

8. Quoted in Keyes, p. 95.

9. Quoted in Keyes, pp. 94–95.

10. Quoted in Keyes, p. 90.

11. This statement is attributed to Mrs. Kirkland's granddaughter, Mrs. Victor Channing Sanborn. Quoted in Keyes, p. 97.

12. "[P]ortraits show her with dark, neat hair; hazel eyes, lively and intelligent in expression," writes Mrs. Knudsen; "her features were strong; lips rather full; about the mouth there is more than a suggestion of determination, as well as of humour." Knudsen, p. 52.

13. Mrs. Sanborn said that Hamilton College would have been called Kirkland College but for the popularity of Alexander Hamilton at the time the charter was issued. This information appears in a note in the Joseph Kirkland Papers.

14. Rufus W. Griswold, *The Prose Writers of America* (Philadelphia, 1847), p. 463.

15. Quoted in Keyes, pp. 105–6.

16. Typescript copy of letter dated London, May 30, 1827, to Caroline Stansbury, in the Joseph Kirkland Papers.

17. *Ibid.*

18. *Ibid.*

19. Typescript copy of letter dated Utica, December 25, 1826, to William Kirkland, in the Joseph Kirkland Papers.

20. "There may be a general idea that learning [in America] is a good thing," Mrs. Kirkland wrote some years later; "but what learning, and what amount of it may be desirable, is quite another question. To read and write and cypher—all tending directly towards advancement in life—must be advantageous to all; this is a conceded point. But one step beyond these, opposition begins. That spontaneous Western question—'*Where's the use?*' always has the very narrowest utilitarian drift. . . . While this . . . sentiment is cherished, anything more than the merest rudiments of education must be of course out of the question."
Although Mrs. Kirkland was expressing an opinion here about public education in the West, she made it clear that her comments reflected a general apathy toward education in the United States: "let us not flatter ourselves . . . that [interest in education] is wanted only in the West." "Forest Literature," *The Union Magazine of Literature and Art,* II (May, 1848), 211–12.

21. See Clyde E. Henson, *Joseph Kirkland* (New Haven, 1962). Mr. Henson's study is published in Twayne's United States Authors Series.

22. "The arrival of Mr. and Mrs. Kirkland to take charge of [the] institution," commented the editor of a Detroit newspaper, "has been immediately followed by the reception of a large number of pupils, and the prospects of the Academy are cheering. . . . The gentleman and lady at the head of it will be enabled by their own experience, and talents . . . to afford instruction to a very large number of pupils, and the accommodations of the beautiful and spacious edifice erected for their use, will be amply sufficient for the comfort and health of all who may avail themselves of the benefit of this institution. We doubt not that the advantages of the Female Academy in this city will be equal to those of any similar institution in the West. . . ." Quoted in Keyes, p. 119.

23. Administering the seminary was probably a difficult task be-

cause of Kirkland's deafness and poor eyesight, and his wife shared the responsibilities, as a news clipping of the day suggests: "Mr Kirkland . . . suffer[ed] under the disadvantage of being . . . deaf and near-sighted. His wife was charming in person and mind, and being possessed of executive ability and considerable force of character, was a worthy helpmate." Quoted in Keyes, p. 141.

"Mrs. Kirkland was a very good teacher and was especially successful in teaching the art of reading," recalled one of her pupils. "Mr. Kirkland was a good teacher, but he was very deaf and the girls used to take advantage of that when they recited to him in Algebra." Quoted in Knudsen, p. 76.

24. The announcement appeared in the Detroit *Journal and Courier*, September 1, 1835. Quoted in Keyes, p. 120.

25. *Western Clearings* (New York, 1846), p. 2.

26. Keyes, p. 123.

27. Quoted in Keyes, p. 155.

28. The children appear in *A New Home*: Elizabeth, eleven, is Alice; Joseph, nine, is Arthur; Cordelia, four, is Bel; William, Jr., six months, is Charlie.

29. An old newspaper account indicates that the Kirklands tried to make the settlers in the town as contented as possible: "both became quite popular. Mr Kirkland was a good friend to the emigrants who settled in his neighborhood. One of his schemes was to help every poor family to bed clothing. He had a number of 'comforters' made, and he loaned them to the new settlers, only requiring that they should be clean when returned. Mrs Kirkland was also prominent in charitable work . . . and was the founder of the Ladies' Beneficent society." Quoted in Keyes, p. 179.

30. *A New Home—Who'll Follow?* (New Haven, 1965), p. 160.

31. *Ibid.*, p. 166.

32. Mrs. Kirkland wrote Rufus W. Griswold: "[My husband] bids me say, with his compliments, that he hopes you will make your letters *longer* instead of shorter— The letters of literary gentlemen have an especial value during a country winter, and my spirits require all sorts of aid in these dull times. So when you can spare an hour we shall always be happy to receive the benefit of it." Letter dated Pinckney, February 20, [18]43, to Griswold, in the Clifton Waller Barrett Library of the University of Virginia Library.

33. Edgar Allan Poe, "The Literati of New York City" in *The Complete Works of Edgar Allan Poe*, ed. James A. Harrison, XV (New York, 1902), 24.

34. William Kirkland, "The West, the Paradise of the Poor," *United States Magazine and Democratic Review*, XV (August, 1844), 188.

35. The *Christian Inquirer* was described as "a religious newspaper

. . . which promised, in [Kirkland's] able hands, to exert a wide and healthful influence in the cause of liberal Christianity." "William Kirkland," *Littell's Living Age,* XI (November 14, 1846), 304.

36. *Forest Life,* I (New York, 1842), 9–10.

37. Letter dated Pinckney, December 15, 1840, to Carey and Hart, in the Clifton Waller Barrett Library of the University of Virginia Library.

38. Letter dated Pinckney, July 25, 1842, to Griswold, in the Clifton Waller Barrett Library of the University of Virginia Library.

39. Letter dated Pinckney, February 20, [18]43, to Griswold, in the Clifton Waller Barrett Library of the University of Virginia Library. The "very sentimental love story"—which she did persuade herself to write—was "The Blighted Heart" published in *Graham's,* XXIII (July, 1843), 1–7, later reprinted as "A Legend of East Rock" in *Autumn Hours;* the "trifle" forwarded with the letter was her mother's "An Incident in Dream-Land"; "Conduct and Consequences: An Autobiography" was also written by her mother.

40. Letter dated Pinckney, March 6, 1843, to Carey and Hart, in the Massachusetts Historical Society.

41. Letter dated New York, March 1, 1844, to Carey and Hart, in the Historical Society of Pennsylvania.

42. She may well have written too for the income such stories provided. "I am busy penning some very dull stories for several publications," she wrote her daughter Elizabeth. "My money comes but slowly, and is wanted long before I get it. Nevertheless, when it *does* come, it is most acceptable, and I know not what we should do without this resource." Letter dated Pinckney, March 17, 1843, to Elizabeth Kirkland. Quoted in Keyes, p. 199.

43. *A New Home,* p. 107.

44. *Forest Life,* I, 26.

45. *Ibid.*

46. A notice for the school is in the Bryant-Godwin Collection, New York Public Library.

47. "My school is not as yet very profitable," Mrs. Kirkland wrote Carey and Hart, "but I hope to make it much more so than writing has ever been to me. I believe the same intellect and the same industry which authorship requires, will pay better when exerted in almost any other way—in our country at least. My mantua-maker makes a much better living by his skill at the needle than I can do by the pen— I mention this not as a special reason for declining your request, but as a general reason for laying aside the pen." Letter dated New York, December 12, [18]43, to Carey and Hart, in the Special Collections, the University of Chicago Library.

48. "William Kirkland," p. 304.

49. "Periodical Reading," *United States Magazine and Democratic Review,* XVI (January, 1845), 61, 59.

50. "Literary Women," *The Union Magazine of Literature and Art,* VI (February, 1850), 150–54; "Lion-Hunting," *The Union Magazine of Literature and Art,* VIII (February, 1851), 111–15.

51. Letter dated New York, March 2, [18]47, to Theodore D. Woolsey, in the Theodore Dwight Woolsey Family Collection, Yale University Library.

52. [William Cullen Bryant], "The Death of Mrs. Kirkland," *Littell's Living Age,* LXXXI (April 30, 1864), 237. The comment appeared in the obituary notice Bryant wrote, reprinted from the New York *Evening Post.*

53. Evert A. and George L. Duyckinck, *Cyclopedia of American Literature,* II (New York, 1855), 562.

54. *Autumn Hours* (New York, 1854), p. 21.

55. *The Book of Home Beauty* (New York, 1852), p. 6.

56. Letter dated New York, March 2, [18]47, to Theodore D. Woolsey.

57. Poe, p. 88.

58. Many of these letters are in the Duyckinck Collection and the Bryant-Godwin Collection, New York Public Library.

59. Letter dated [New York], February 19, [1852], to Ralph Waldo Emerson, in the Widener Library, Harvard University Library.

60. Letter dated [New York?], August 3, [1862], in the Johns Hopkins University Library.

61. [Bryant], p. 237.

Chapter Two

1. *A New Home—Who'll Follow?* (New Haven, 1965), p. 31. Subsequent references are to this edition of *A New Home,* with an introduction by William S. Osborne and published in the Masterworks of Literature Series, College and University Press. This edition of the book follows the text of the second edition (1840), incorporating the minor revisions of the first edition which Mrs. Kirkland made. Hereafter, *New Home* (1965), with page reference.

2. In the fall before her marriage Mrs. Kirkland accompanied her aunt on a trip through the Mohawk region of New York State. The trip itself was of no particular consequence; however, a letter she wrote to William Kirkland reveals those traits of writing that were to mark her Western sketches a few years later—the playful depicting of character, the briskly written anecdote, the personal incident enlivened by lurking humor, even the sprinkling of French phrases.

You will probably wonder . . . that I should address you already and from this little Dutch village far from the end of our journey—but comment faire? If I feel like writing, I can do it quite as well when I have nothing to say as when I have something of the greatest importance, and it seems unnecessary to control the inclination when I know my dear Willie will be satisfied with whatever I send him. I hate to fill up my letter with details, but I must give you some account of our journey thus far. We reached no further than Little Falls on Sunday evening. There we found a house full of stage Passengers, and among the rest Mr. Jacob Van den Heuvel of New York—a bachelor of three and forty, rolling in wealth, and one of the most singular beings in existence. Some years ago, when he had almost made up his mind to commit matrimony, he whispered tenderly in the ear of a pretty young *bas bleu* with whom he was desperately enamoured, "Amo te, Maria"—the young lady laughed in his face, and from that time he has never held up his head in the presence of the "fair sex." We left Little Falls the next morning and reached Dockstader's, a tavern about 3 miles west of Caughnawaga, just at nightfall. The landlord was a most curious old German and his wife and daughters as primitive creatures as you ever saw. We were favored with the company of the landlord's "two gals" in our lodging room, and after the noisy barroom became silent for the night, an outrageous cat, which was shut up in the chamber above us, commenced howling most horribly, as well as jumping and scratching in every direction. This serenade continued throughout the night, so that when lights were brought for us to dress by in the morning, we were but little refreshed by our broken slumbers. We had hardly rode a mile before our carriage went over—the hind wheel having come off, in consequence of the breaking of the axle tree. Mr. M. immediately sprang to the horses' heads, and we crawled out as best we might. After a little consultation we concluded to walk on to the next house leaving Mr. M. to take care of the wreck.— The house proved to be a large one containing three families.— The first room I put my head into presented such a congregation of horrors of sight and smell that I was fain to shut the door as speedily as possible. In the next, we found a young woman, apparently not more than eighteen years of age, with a boy of nine months, who walked at least as well as poor Julia did at two years. I felt mortified by the contrast but still the baby interested me—especially as it took such a fancy to me that it would insist on putting its little greasy pads all over the lap of my dress, and making me play with it whether I would or not.— Finding our carriage would be some time in mending, I took a pair of stockings from my sack and very philosophically sat down and darned them completely, while Aunt Mott read the newspaper to me. Then I set off and walked down to the Blacksmith's (half a mile) to see how the carriage came on. Finding there was still much to do, I trudged back to the house, and seeing our hostess very much engaged in sewing, I sat down and helped her until everything was once more ready for a start. This was about twelve o'clock. At two we stopped to dine, some few miles East of Caughnawaga, and after a good cup of coffee, flanked by a substantial beefsteak and some fine potatoes, we set out for this place which we reached before dark, and where we are to have our supper of oysters, which we meant to have eaten this night in Schenectady. We have not accomplished any great distance but I have enjoyed the ride very highly. . . . Mr. M. is the most attentive of beaux, and leaves nothing undone which can contribute to our comfort. My dear love, I never thought of you oftener or with more tenderness than during these three days, and I comfort myself by thinking that the image of your absent Caroline has been not infrequently the partner of your silent hours.

"Tu serais ingrat si tu ne l'aimais pas."

Letter dated Amsterdam, November 20, 1827, to William Kirkland. Quoted in Keyes, pp. 111–12.

3. See *New Home* (1965), pp. 42–43, for Mrs. Kirkland's amusing account of how the village was named.

4. Mrs. Kirkland wrote an editor some years later: "I little thought of becoming an author before I lived in the wilderness— There, the strange things I saw and heard every day prompted me to description, for they always presented themselves to me under a humorous aspect — Finding my letters amusing to my friends, I thought of 'more of the same sort' for a book—but always felt any serious doubts whether it would be possible to find a publisher for such stuff— A friend in N.Y. however was more hopeful—and in due time 'A New Home' saw the light under the auspices of Mr Francis of this city. Success of course induced another attempt, and Forest Life was published." Letter dated New York, January 18, 1857, to John S. Hart, in the Cornell University Library.

5. *New Home* (1965), p. 36.

6. *Ibid.*, p. 38.

7. *Ibid.*, pp. 82–83.

8. Percy H. Boynton, *The Rediscovery of the Frontier* (Chicago, 1931), pp. 176–77.

9. Charles Fenno Hoffman, *A Winter in the West*, I (New York, 1835), 109–13 *passim*.

10. *Ibid.*, I, 183–84.

11. *Ibid.*, I, 191, 219.

12. Hoffman wondered why "the tempting-looking oak opening" (marshy land) was often avoided by the more wary emigrant who "erect[ed] his dwelling in the thick forest." *Ibid.*, I, 154.

13. *Ibid.*, I, 153.

14. Washington Irving, *A Tour on the Prairies* (Norman, 1962), p. 51. Irving's book is edited for the modern reader, with an introductory essay and textual notes by John Francis McDermott in the Western Frontier Library, published by the University of Oklahoma Press.

15. *Ibid.*, p. 34.

16. *Ibid.*, p. 85.

17. *Ibid.*, pp. 21–24 *passim*, 32.

18. *Ibid.*, p. 41.

19. Boynton, p. 177.

20. Alexander Cowie, *The Rise of the American Novel* (New York, 1948), p. 219.

21. James Hall, *Legends of the West* (Philadelphia, 1832), p. 172.

22. Letter dated [New York], April 8, [?], to E. A. Duyckinck, in the Duyckinck Collection, New York Public Library.

A great number of articles in the early volumes of the *Michigan Pioneer Collections* (the periodical of the Michigan Historical Society) attest to the validity of Mrs. Kirkland's picture of the Michigan wilderness in the 1830's; and Mrs. Louise N. Knudsen in her thesis "Caroline Kirkland, Pioneer" draws on many Michigan sources to substantiate the accuracy of Mrs. Kirkland's picture.

23. See Mrs. Kirkland's comments on the destruction of the wilderness in *Forest Life*, I (New York, 1842), 43–47. Hereafter, *Forest Life*, with volume number and page reference.

24. *New Home* (1965), p. 63.

25. *Ibid.*

26. *Ibid.*, p. 64.

27. *Forest Life*, I, 210–11.

28. *New Home* (1965), p. 85.

29. *Ibid.*, p. 177.

30. Quoted in Keyes, p. 187.

31. Letter from William Thompson dated Rose, Oakland County, Michigan, March 8, 1843, to a member of his family, in the Michigan Historical Collections of the University of Michigan.

32. *New Home* (1965), pp. 102, 103.

33. William Kirkland, "The West, the Paradise of the Poor," *United States Magazine and Democratic Review*, XV (August, 1844), 184.

34. *New Home* (1965), p. 53.

35. "The West, the Paradise of the Poor," p. 182.

36. *Ibid.*, p. 184.

37. *Ibid.*, pp. 189–90 *passim*.

38. *New Home* (1965), pp. 71–72.

39. *Ibid.*, p. 228.

40. *Ibid.*, pp. 113–14.

41. *Ibid.*, pp. 148–49 *passim*.

42. *Ibid.*, p. 230.

43. One village idler was Simeon Jenkins, the backwoods politician, the earnest patriot so anxious to avoid an honest day's work that he would take any office "that's in the gift o' the people." He changed his party, and his political beliefs, to insure his continuing in office—arguing that "any man that's too proud to serve his country ain't fit to live." *New Home* (1965), p. 213. Mrs. Kirkland introduced him again in *Forest Life*, still trying to hoodwink the electorate: "our old neighbor had been sadly unsuccessful in the many ingenious modes by which he had attempted to get a living without work. . . . He is one of a numerous class who solace themselves by decrying worldly advantages which they have not been able to attain, and habits of neatness and refinement which contravene their own coarse and self-indulgent usages. They are self-deceivers undoubtedly, but they seldom deceive others. Their inconsistencies invariably tell the truth." *Forest Life*, I, 157–58.

44. *New Home* (1965), pp. 227–29 *passim*.

45. *Ibid.*, p. 180.

46. "I am aware that I have . . . been adventurous, far beyond the bounds of prudence," she admitted near the end of the book. *Ibid.*, p. 230.

47. *Forest Life*, I, 5.

48. *Ibid.*, II, 230–31.

49. Rufus W. Griswold, *The Prose Writers of America* (Philadelphia, 1847), p. 463.

50. "A New Home—Who'll Follow? or, Glimpses of Western Life by Mrs. Mary Clavers—an actual settler," New York *Mirror*, XVII (October 12, 1839), 127.

51. "*A New Home; Who'll Follow? or, Glimpses of Western Life* by Mrs. Mary Clavers, an Actual Settler," *North American Review*, L (January, 1840), 206–23 *passim*.

52. "*A New Home: Who'll Follow? or, Glimpses of Western Life* Mrs. Mary Clavers, an Actual Settler," *Knickerbocker Magazine*, XIV (November, 1839), 452.

53. "A New Home—Who'll Follow? or, Glimpses of Western Life," *Literary Gazette*, No. 1190 (November 9, 1839), 713.

54. "A New Home—Who'll Follow? or, Glimpses of Western Life," *Athenaeum*, No. 635 (December 28, 1839), 981–82 *passim*.

55. Edgar Allan Poe, "The Literati of New York City" in *The Complete Works of Edgar Allan Poe*, ed. James A. Harrison, XV (New York, 1902), 84–86 *passim*.

56. Griswold, p. 463.

Chapter Three

1. *Forest Life*, I, 10.

2. *Ibid.*

3. "Forest Life," *Knickerbocker Magazine*, XX (August, 1842), 188–91 *passim*.

4. "Forest Life," *United States Magazine and Democratic Review*, XI (August, 1842), 216–17.

5. [Edgar Allan Poe], "Forest Life," *Broadway Journal*, I (February 1, 1845), 77.

6. "Forest Life," *North American Review*, LV (October, 1842), 512–13 *passim*.

7. "Forest Life," *Graham's Magazine*, XXI (September, 1842), 153. The reviewer compared Mrs. Kirkland with Mary Russell Mitford, saying that she was "infinitely superior" to Miss Mitford as a "delineator of . . . rural life." Mrs. Kirkland wrote in the preface to *A New Home* that Miss Mitford's sketches of English village life had suggested to her the composition her stories about Western life would take.

8. "Mrs. Kirkland's 'Western Clearings,'" *Littell's Living Age*, VIII (March 14, 1846), 506. The review is copied from the London *Spectator*.

9. "Mrs. Kirkland's 'Western Clearings,'" *Littell's Living Age*, IX (June 13, 1846), 528. The review is copied from *Chambers' Journal*.

10. "Mrs. Kirkland's 'Western Clearings,'" *Littell's Living Age*, VII (December 6, 1845), 442. The review is copied from the Boston *Courier*.

11. [William Cullen Bryant], "Mrs. Kirkland's 'Western Clearings,'" *Littell's Living Age*, VII (December 6, 1845), 442. The review is copied from the New York *Evening Post*.

12. [Edgar Allan Poe], "Western Clearings," *Broadway Journal*, II (November 29, 1845), 320.

13. *Forest Life*, II, 233.

14. *Ibid.*, II, 232.

15. *Ibid.*, I, 5.

16. *Ibid.*, II, 45.
17. *Ibid.*, I, 32.
18. *Ibid.*, I, 34.
19. *Ibid.*, I, 31.
20. *Ibid.*, I, 33.
21. *Ibid.*, I, 209.
22. *Ibid.*, I, 114.
23. *Ibid.*, I, 122.
24. *Ibid.*, I, 19–24 *passim.*
25. *Ibid.*, I, 36.
26. *Ibid.*, I, 49–50.
27. *New Home* (1965), p. 188.
28. *Forest Life*, II, 184, 190.
29. *Ibid.*, II, 190.
30. *Ibid.*, I, 90.
31. *New Home* (1965), p. 225.
32. *Forest Life*, II, 166.
33. *Ibid.*, I, 153.
34. *New Home* (1965), p. 158.
35. *Forest Life*, I, 43.
36. *Ibid.*, I, 38.
37. *Ibid.*, I, 41.
38. *Ibid.*, I, 42.
39. *Ibid.*, I, 27–28 *passim.*
40. *Ibid.*, I, 37–38.
41. *Ibid.*, I, 52.
42. *New Home* (1965), p. 118.
43. *Forest Life*, I, 52.
44. *Ibid.*
45. *Ibid.*, I, 203.
46. *Ibid.*, II, 99.
47. *Ibid.*, II, 144–45.
48. *Ibid.*, I, 167.
49. *New Home* (1965), pp. 184–85.
50. *Forest Life*, I, 60.
51. *Ibid.*, I, 11.
52. *Ibid.*, I, 36.
53. *Ibid.*, I, 110–11.
54. *Ibid.*, II, 148.
55. *Ibid.*, II, 159–60.
56. *New Home* (1965), p. 224.
57. *Ibid.*, p. 79.
58. *Forest Life*, I, 31.
59. *Ibid.*, I, 139.

60. *New Home* (1965), pp. 218–19 *passim*.
61. *Ibid.*, p. 219.
62. *Ibid.*
63. *Forest Life*, I, 226.
64. *Ibid.*, I, 123.
65. *Ibid.*, II, 148.
66. *New Home* (1965), p. 72.
67. *Forest Life*, I, 96.
68. *Ibid.*, I, 107.
69. *New Home* (1965), p. 86.
70. *Forest Life*, I, 109.
71. *Ibid.*, I, 156–57 *passim*.
72. *Ibid.*, I, 205–6.
73. *Ibid.*, I, 13.
74. *New Home* (1965), p. 228.
75. George Core (ed.), *Regionalism and Beyond: Essays of Randall Stewart* (Nashville, 1968), p. 161.
76. Letter dated New York, May 19, 1844, to Carey and Hart, in the Boston Public Library.
77. *Western Clearings* (New York, 1846), p. vi. Hereafter, *Western Clearings*, with page reference.
78. See in *Western Clearings* the following essays and sketches: "The Land-Fever"; "Ball at Thram's Huddle"; "A Forest Fete"; "Love vs. Aristocracy"; "The Bee-Tree"; "Idle People"; "Ambuscades" and "The Schoolmaster's Progress." Some of this material had been published previously in magazines: "Recollections of the Land-Fever," *Knickerbocker Magazine*, XVI (September, 1840), 205–12; "Ball at Thram's Huddle: A Pencil Sketch," *Knickerbocker Magazine*, XV (April, 1840), 325–31; "A Forest Fete," *Knickerbocker Magazine*, XVII (April, 1841), 276–80; "Love vs. Aristocracy: Or Shill-I, Shall-I?" *Graham's Magazine*, XXIV (March, 1844), 116–23.
79. *Western Clearings*, p. 217.
80. *Ibid.*, p. 38.
81. *Ibid.*, p. 54.
82. *Ibid.*, pp. 66–72 *passim*.
83. *Ibid.*, pp. 168–70 *passim*.
84. *Ibid.*, p. vi.
85. Quoted in Randolph C. Randall, *James Hall: Spokesman of the New West* (Columbus, Ohio, 1964), p. 276. Letter dated April 20, 1846, to Wiley and Putnam, in the New York Public Library.
86. *Western Clearings*, p. 213.
87. *Forest Life*, II, 171.
88. *Ibid.*, II, 182.
89. *Western Clearings*, p. vi.

90. *Forest Life,* I, 115–16.

91. *New Home* (1965), p. 214.

92. Keyes, p. 244.

Chapter Four

1. Caroline M. Kirkland, "Editorial Miscellany," *The Union Magazine of Literature and Art,* II (April, 1848), 191. Hereafter, title of article, *Union,* volume number, and page reference.

2. Letter dated Wednesday, June 18, [1847], to E. A. Duyckinck, in the Duyckinck Collection. There are a number of Mrs. Kirkland's letters in this collection.

3. Letter dated New York, May 15, 1847, to [Bryant], in the Bryant-Godwin Collection.

4. William Kirkland, "British and American Monthlies," *Godey's Magazine and Lady's Book,* XXX (June, 1845), 273.

5. "Introductory," *Union,* I, 1, 2.

6. Letter dated New York, January 19, 1848, to [?], in the Cornell University Library.

7. See Frank Luther Mott, *A History of American Magazines, 1741–1850,* I (Cambridge, 1957), 769–72.

8. Letter dated [New York], August 24, [18]47, to Bryant, in the Bryant-Godwin Collection.

9. Letter dated New York, September 22, [18]47, to Longfellow, in the Widener Library, Harvard University Library.

10. Letter dated New York, November 16, 1847, to Taylor, in the Cornell University Library.

11. Letter dated New York, December 9, [1847], to Willis, in the Massachusetts Historical Society.

12. Letter dated Tuesday morning, [October, 1847?], to E. A. Duyckinck, in the Duyckinck Collection.

13. Letter dated [New York], March 31, [1848], to Post, in the Cornell University Library.

14. Letter dated [New York], January 15, [18]48, to [?], in the Clifton Waller Barrett Library of the University of Virginia Library.

15. Letter dated New York, January 8, 1848, to a Western correspondent, a Mrs. Norris, in the Michigan Historical Collections of the University of Michigan.

16. Letter dated Birmingham, April 27, 1848, to Taylor, in the Cornell University Library. Correspondence relating to the first European trip is deposited in the Cornell University Library.

17. Letter dated London, May 17, 1848, to Taylor, in the Cornell University Library.

18. Letter dated Rome, June 29, 1848, to Taylor, in the Cornell University Library.

19. "Editorial," *Union*, IV, 75.

20. A number of these letters informing Hart of her correspondence are deposited in the Cornell University Library.

21. Letter dated [New York], March 30, 1849, to Lowell, in the Widener Library, Harvard University Library.

22. Letters dated [New York, March 25, 1849?], and New York, May 3, 1849, to Hart, in the Cornell University Library.

23. Letter dated New York, October 27, 1849, to Hart, in the Cornell University Library.

24. Letter dated New York, June 7, 1850, to [Hart and Sartain], in the Cornell University Library.

25. Letter dated New York, March 30, 1849, to [John G. Saxe?], in the Miscellaneous Manuscript Collection, New York Public Library. She was writing the two-volume record of the trip to Europe and an introduction to Mrs. Mary Eastman's *Dahcotah* and soliciting articles for the *Christian Inquirer*. She asked Lowell to contribute to the newspaper, "that dear child of my soul's adoption." Letter dated [New York], March 30, 1849, to Lowell, in the Widener Library, Harvard University Library.

26. Letter dated Roslyn, [New York], September 13, 1849, to Bowen, in the Charles Roberts Autograph Collection, Haverford College Library, Haverford, Pennsylvania.

27. The Western Sketches appearing in the first two volumes of the *Union* are "The Village School" (July, 1847); "Harvest" (August, 1847); "The Justice" (September, 1847); "The Country Funeral" (October, 1847); "Steps to Ruin" (November, 1847); "The Singing School" (December, 1847); "The Hard Winter" (January, 1848); "A Love of a Singing Master" (March, 1848); "Sunday in the Country" (April, 1848); "Forest Literature" (May, 1848); "The Log-House" (June, 1848). Two later sketches are "Bush-Life" (January, 1850) and "The Log School-house" (April, 1850).

28. Letter dated New York, November 11, 1848, to Mrs. Norris, in the Michigan Historical Collections of the University of Michigan.

29. *The Evening Book or, Fireside Talk on Morals and Manners, with Sketches of Western Life* (New York, 1853), pp. 278–88 *passim*. Hereafter, *Evening Book*, with page reference.

30. "The Justice," *Union*, I, 114–15 *passim*.

31. "The Hard Winter," *Union*, II, 43.

32. "Sunday in the Country," *Union*, II, 166–67 *passim*.

33. See Note 20, Chapter One.

34. *Evening Book*, pp. 302–5.

35. *Ibid.*, pp. 135–37 *passim*.

36. *Ibid.*, pp. 183–84 *passim*.

37. "Editorial," *Union*, IV, 222.

38. "Sight-seeing in Europe" [No. 1], *Union*, III, 4.
39. "Sight-seeing in Europe" [No. 2], *Union*, III, 50.
40. "Sight-seeing in Europe" [No. 3], *Union*, III, 147.
41. *Ibid.*, p. 149.
42. "Sight-seeing in Europe" [No. 4], *Union*, III, 195–99 *passim*.
43. "Sight-seeing in Europe" [No. 5], *Union*, III, 242–44 *passim*.
44. "Sight-seeing in Europe" [No. 6], *Union*, IV, 60–61.
45. *Ibid.*, p. 61.
46. "Sight-seeing in Europe" [No. 7], *Union*, IV, 183.
47. Letter dated New York, November 11, 1848, to Mrs. Norris, in the Michigan Historical Collections of the University of Michigan.
48. Letter dated Rome, June 29, 1848, to Taylor, in the Cornell University Library.
49. She was disturbed by the preference for Catholicism that a young English girl had shown when she had become a convert and then a nun in a French convent. "She said she would pray for us," Mrs. Kirkland told her readers, "having been shocked at finding we were Protestant,—while we, on our part, would gladly have converted . . . [her] to a faith which would allow her the full use of her fine natural powers." "Sight-seeing in Europe" [No. 5], *Union*, III, 245.
50. "Detached Thoughts about England," *Union*, IV, 127–28.
51. *Ibid.*, p. 129.
52. "English and American Manners," *Union*, IV, 403.
53. "New York" [No. 1], *Union*, IX, 149.
54. "New York" [No. 2], *Union*, IX, 204.
55. In an editorial comment, she gave a little history of the poem —mentioning that the early version illustrated "the gradual development of an idea in the mind of a man of original genius. This poem came into our possession about a year since . . . [consisting] of eighteen lines!" "Editorial," *Union*, IV, 386–87.
56. Hart, not Mrs. Kirkland, wrote that he was somewhat embarrassed to discover the poem *"which we had bought and paid for"* had been printed earlier in the newspapers. "Editorial," *Union*, VI, 99.
57. "Books of the Month," *Union*, I, 191.
58. ["Note to Correspondents"], *Union*, II, 96.
59. "Books of the Month," *Union*, I, 286.
60. "Books of the Month," *Union*, II, 46.
61. ["Books of the Month"], *Union*, V, 64.
62. "Books of the Month," *Union*, II, 142.
63. Letter dated New York, November 7, 1848, to Hart, in the Cornell University Library.
64. ["Books of the Month"], *Union*, V, 320. She alluded to *Omoo* in an editorial comment, referring to Melville's "censures of the mis-

sionaries at the Sandwich Islands." "Editorial Miscellany," *Union*, I, 96.

65. ["Books of the Month"], *Union*, V, 126.

66. ["Books of the Month"], *Union*, VI, 174.

67. Letter dated [New York], March 26, [1850], to [?], in the Widener Library, Harvard University Library.

68. Mrs. Kirkland is with good company, in spite of Barrett Wendell's comment: "to close our first survey of the literature produced in the Middle States[,] there are certain names which we might have mentioned; Mrs. Kirkland . . . whom Poe records among the Literati, wrote some sketches of life in the Middle West which are still vivid, and although of slight positive merit, decidedly interesting as history. Hermann [*sic*] Melville, with his books about the South Seas . . . and with his novels of maritime adventure, began a career of literary promise, which never came to fruition." Barrett Wendell, *A Literary History of America*, 5th ed. (New York, 1909), p. 229.

Chapter Five

1. *Evening Book*, pp. x-xi *passim*.

2. *Ibid.*, p. ix.

3. "The Town Poor: A Western Reminiscence," *Arthur's Ladies' Magazine*, VI (January, 1846), 44–47.

4. *Evening Book*, p. 277.

5. *Ibid.*, p. 198.

6. *A Book for the Home Circle; or, Familiar Thoughts on Various Topics, Literary, Moral and Social* (New York, 1853), pp. x-xi. Hereafter, *Home Circle*, with page reference.

7. *Ibid.*, p. 110.

8. *Ibid.*, pp. 19–23 *passim*.

9. Mary Eastman, *Dahcotah; or, Life and Legends of the Sioux around Fort Snelling* (New York, 1849), pp. vi-xi *passim*.

10. Marian Reid, *Woman, Her Education and Influence* (New York, [1848]), p. 22.

11. "The condition of the women of the present-day seems to bear no little resemblance to that of the unfortunate hens in the basket of the poulterer,—restless, crowded and uncomfortable; evincing, ever and anon, by a faint, uneasy chirping, a desire for wider bounds, and occasionally risking strangulation by a spasmodic effort, which only forces the aspiring head through a mesh in the strong netting, occasions a great clacking among the sisterhood, and earns a rap on the pate from the hard-hearted owner." *Ibid.*, p. 9.

12. *Spenser and the Faery Queen* (New York, 1847), p. vii.

13. Keyes, p. 306.

14. Letter dated Washington, July 15, 1855, to [Jared Sparks?], in the Boston Public Library.

15. *Personal Memoirs of George Washington* (New York, 1857), p. 9.

16. *Ibid.*, pp. 36–38.

17. *Ibid.*, p. 45.

18. She was sometimes embarrassed by Washington's personal habits, feeling the need to explain or justify them to her young readers. On gambling—"'At home all day at cards—it snowing.' [entry in Diary] In those days cards had not yet been proscribed, as they are in ours. Washington seems to have played occasionally, but was evidently quite indifferent about it; he probably resorted to a game as the easiest way of entertaining company, shut up in a lonely country-house through an impracticable storm. Mr. Custis says that he played only whist, and in later and more anxious times discarded even that." (*Ibid.*, p. 204.) On drinking—"The 'Temperance cause,' as such, had never been heard of, in his day, and he, like all the world, thought the use of wine and other liquors as proper and necessary as that of milk or bread. He always used them, whether to his benefit or injury it is difficult to say, but probably without ever speculating on the subject. Perhaps the green tea he was so fond of, and which he drank at breakfast and in the evening, may have done him more harm than the 'two or three glasses of good wine' that we know he took after dinner, or the occasional stronger potations his minutely kept accounts tell us that he used, on his journeys and other occasions." (*Ibid.*, pp. 205–6.) On dipping snuff—"Perhaps . . . this was only for the use of visitors, whose boxes might happen to be empty during some of those long snow-storms that throw people upon their vices." (*Ibid.*, p. 209.)

19. "Mrs. Kirkland's Travels," *The Literary World,* IV (June 2, 1849), 472.

20. *Home Circle*, p. xi.

21. This discussion of Mrs. Kirkland's "theory" is simply a supplement to her opinions on writing and writers already expressed elsewhere in the study.

22. *Forest Life*, I, 222.

23. "Books of the Month," *Union*, I, 142.

24. *Home Circle*, p. 35.

25. *Ibid.*, p. 45.

26. *Ibid.*, p. 87.

27. *Ibid.*, pp. 82, 83.

28. "Introductory," *Union*, I, 1.

29. "Sense, Common and Uncommon" in *Home Circle*, p. 162.

30. *Ibid.,* p. 19.

31. *Evening Book,* p. x.

32. *Ibid.,* p. 64.

33. *Ibid.,* p. 49.

34. *Ibid.,* p. 18.

35. *Ibid.,* p. 97.

36. *Home Circle,* p. 142.

37. *Evening Book,* pp. 128–29.

38. "Vincent Hervey, or the Man of Impulse," *The Columbian Lady's and Gentleman's Magazine,* II (August, 1844), 49–55.

39. "The Belles of Etherington," *The Columbian Lady's and Gentleman's Magazine,* I (March, 1844), 125–30.

40. "Editorial Miscellany," *Broadway Journal,* II (September 27, 1845), 184; Briggs is quoted in Fred Lewis Pattee, *The Feminine Fifties* (New York, 1940), p. 261.

41. "Prison Association," *Broadway Journal,* II (July 26, 1845), 45. One of Mrs. Kirkland's active charities was work in rehabilitating discharged women convicts. She wrote a tract—*The Helping Hand* (1853)—imploring contributions to the cause.

42. "The Devices of Beggary," *Broadway Journal,* I (February 1, 1845), 72–73; "City Amusements," I (February 22, 1845), 120–21; "Reform," I (April 19, 1845), 243; "On Writing for Magazines," I (May 10, 1845), 291–93.

43. Briggs declared that, since the purpose of *Putnam's* was to encourage new writers, contributors' names would be withheld: "each article might stand on its own merits, and the young unknown be presented . . . on a perfect equality with the illustrious contributor whose name, alone, would give him an audience." "Editorial," *Putnam's Monthly,* I (June, 1853), 704.

44. "How They Manage in Europe," *Putnam's Monthly,* I (April, 1853), 427–36; "The Benevolent Institution of New York," I (June, 1853), 673–86; "Educational Institutions of New York," II (July, 1853), 1–16; "Academies and Universities," II (August, 1853), 169–79; "What Impressions Do We, and Should We, Make Abroad?" II (October, 1853), 345–54; "Washington's Early Days" [No. 1], III (January, 1854), 1–10; "Washington's Early Days" [No. 2], III (February, 1854), 121–34; "Places of Public Amusement," III (February, 1854), 141–52; "Manners," III (June, 1854), 609–14.

45. Letter dated Roslyn, [New York], September 13, 1849, to Bowen, in the Charles Roberts Autograph Collection, Haverford College Library.

46. "The Great Prairie State," *The Continental Monthly Magazine,* III (May, 1863), 513–19; "Town or Country?," *The Prairie Chicken,* No. 9 (June 1, 1865), 4; "Concerts," No. 10 (July 1, 1865), 3; "Essay

on Works of Fiction: Written as a Preface to an Unpublished Novel,"
No. 11 (August 1, 1865), 4.

47. "Town or Country?," *The Prairie Chicken,* No. 9 (June 1,
1865), 4.

48. Undated letter to Parke Godwin, in Bryant-Godwin Collection.

49. Letter dated [New York], April 29, 1849, to [?], in the Cornell
University Library.

50. Letter dated Wednesday, the 3rd [?], to E. A. Duyckinck, in
the Duyckinck Collection.

51. ". . . teaching," she wrote a correspondent, "seems to me very
dependent on personal qualifications—a teacher, like a poet, must be
born, not made—and therefore the *system* adopted does not appear
to me of the *first* importance but only secondary. In public schools,
where teaching is on the wholesale plan—not addressed so particularly to individual minds, it is different. And as I am not naturally
systematic, I may be wholly wrong in my appreciation of the importance of particular plans in teaching. Intelligence—information, and
a good degree of personal magnetism, with quick sympathies, seem
to me all important." Letter dated New York, August 10, [18]61, to
Theodore Weld, in the University of Michigan Library.

52. "New York" [No. 2], *Union,* IX (September, 1851), 205.

53. Letter dated Danville, Illinois, April 4, 1863, to "Edmund
Kirke," editor of *The Continental Monthly,* in the Johns Hopkins University Library.

54. Letter dated New York, February 1, 1864, to Halleck, in the
Massachusetts Historical Society.

Chapter Six

1. Letter dated New York, March 10, 1857, to [Hart], in the Historical Society of Pennsylvania.

2. John S. Hart, *Female Prose Writers of America* (Philadelphia,
1852), p. 106.

3. "A Day in the Life of a Lady Editor," *Arthur's Home Magazine,*
III(April, 1854), 314. The article is copied from *Mother's Journal.*

4. How earnest she was in the essays and sentimental fiction is indicated in the kind of letter she once wrote her daughter Elizabeth, who
had left Michigan for school in the East:

Your [letter] . . . gave us much pleasure—being written with a
freedom and amplitude which your letters do not always evince.
I hope you will cultivate a habit of expressing your thoughts
frankly and gracefully on paper—few things will be more improving to yourself or more agreeable to your friends. To be a
really good and satisfactory correspondent requires not only a

warm heart and well-stored head, but a considerable amount of effort and self-command—since a good correspondent does not only write by fits and starts, but whenever the time comes and as much as the occasion requires. This is not always pleasant in itself—but the habit on the whole is one which contributes in no small degree to the general happiness, sympathy and good will. . . .

To make a young lady all she should be, she must watch her air, her gait, her mode of sitting, of speaking, of entering a room, of addressing persons of different ages and stations—all are necessary to perfect good breeding, and manners which will speak for her in any company. You may remember I told you at Cleveland that you were lacking in *tact* in your manner of addressing people older than yourself. You were apt to be rather familiar and vulgar in your attempts to be friendly—not that you did not *feel* proper respect, but that you had not studied the true art of making your manner express your real feelings. This was to be expected as the consequence of associating so long with people whose manners are very incorrect—but I hope you have amended this long ago. A flippant and forward air is one of the most disgusting to well bred people. Too much reserve is far preferable. You must not set down these things as trifles. They are all worthy of attention and effort; and far from detracting from the solid excellence which must be your highest aim, they aid in recommending worth, and increasing its influence. It has been said that "whoever makes goodness disagreeable commits high treason against virtue." Agreeable manners with a pious and benevolent heart, make the perfection of human nature. Indeed, the full and true influence of enlightened religious feeling produces the only truly consistent grace of manner—for it includes everything that can add to the happiness of mankind. . . .

[D]on't be *sharp* upon your cousins as I fear you are a little inclined to be. A sharp, satirical tongue! Oh what a blemish in the character of a young woman whose gentle influences should contribute only to peace and good will!

Letter dated Pinckney, February 25, [1843], to Elizabeth Kirkland. Quoted in Keyes, pp. 196–97.

5. A review of *The Evening Book*, appearing in the Duyckincks' *Literary World*, summarizes the polite sentiments women readers and friendly reviewers held for Mrs. Kirkland:

We have often called attention to Mrs. Kirkland's Conversational Essays in the magazines, a mingling of description, home and travelled observations with touches of character, which form one of the most agreeable and withal profitable literary entertainments of the day. Her opinions on social topics are generally sound and always on the side of nature, and what she happily claims as the "humanity" of the subject; now and then on more indifferent conventional matters we fancy her taking the whim or humor of the moment for a guide. . . .

The Evening Book is filled with all these best traits of Mrs. Kirkland's genius we have just alluded to. . . . The spirit in which these subjects are handled is always intelligent and always feminine. There is no pretence of style, the sentences running on with an easy charm, not below the dignities and not insensible to the levities of the occasion.

It is a book withal of true American life, in which, while nothing is obtruded upon us, everything requisite is insensibly felt. In a city of growing wealth and extravagance and, almost of necessity, corresponding heartlessness, Mrs. Kirkland asserts the worth of plain living, agreeable facilities of intercourse, [a]nd enlivening mental cultivation. In truth there is in this *Evening Book* a key to personal and social happiness in America, well worth perusing. The public certainly owes a cordial recognition to this most agreeable and instructive volume.

"Mrs. Kirkland's Evening Book," *The Literary World,* IX (November 29, 1851), 429.

6. "Mrs. Kirkland's 'Western Clearings,' " *Littell's Living Age,* VII (December 6, 1845), 441. This comment appears in Taylor's review of *Western Clearings,* a review copied from the New York *Tribune.*

7. *Forest Life,* I, 14.

8. "Tales of the South and West," *United States Magazine and Democratic Review,* XVIII (June, 1846), 472–73. This comment appears in a review in which the writer discusses *Western Clearings,* Hall's *The Wilderness and the War-Path,* and Simms's *The Wigwam and the Cabin.*

9. Quoted in Henson, p. 88.

10. Henson, p. 89.

11. "The difficulty in [the] realistic novel," Joseph Kirkland declared, "is in knowing what to omit. Much detail is good. Too much detail is intolerable." He strongly objected to the French realists Flaubert and Zola because their fiction was indecent: writers ought not concern themselves with the sordid aspects of life, nor with the animal drives that were said to motivate individuals. "*Let only truth be told, and not all the truth,*" he wrote later in an essay on realism. Quoted in Henson, pp. 79, 87.

See also George Monteiro, "A Note on the Realism of Joseph Kirkland," *American Literary Realism 1870–1910*, II (Spring, 1969), 77–78. Monteiro cites a heretofore unpublished letter of Kirkland which "anticipates by some six years . . . the credo for literary realism he was to announce in the *Dial* (Chicago) in 1893."

Selected Bibliography

PRIMARY SOURCES

1. Books

Autumn Hours, and Fireside Reading. New York: Charles Scribner, 1854.

A Book for the Home Circle; or, Familiar Thoughts on Various Topics, Literary, Moral and Social. New York: Charles Scribner, 1853.

The Book of Home Beauty. New York: G. P. Putnam and Company, 1852.

The Evening Book or, Fireside Talk on Morals and Manners, with Sketches of Western Life. New York: Charles Scribner, 1852.

Forest Life. 2 Vols. New York: C. S. Francis and Company, 1842.

Garden Walks with the Poets. New York: G. P. Putnam and Company, 1852.

The Helping Hand, Comprising an Account of the Home for Discharged Female Convicts and an Appeal in Behalf of That Institution. New York: Charles Scribner, 1853.

Holidays Abroad; or, Europe from the West. 2 Vols. New York: Baker and Scribner, 1849.

A New Home—Who'll Follow? New Haven: College and University Press, 1965.

Personal Memoirs of George Washington. New York: D. Appleton and Company, 1857.

The School-Girl's Garland. New York: Charles Scribner, 1864.

Spenser and the Faery Queen. New York: Wiley and Putnam, 1847.

Western Clearings. New York: Wiley and Putnam, 1846.

2. Articles

(An abbreviated title of the magazine is used after the first bibliographical entry.)

"An Apology for Authors," *Knickerbocker Magazine,* XIX (February, 1842), 97–102.

"The Art of Dreaming," *Godey's Magazine and Lady's Book,* XXXIV (June, 1847), 287–89.

"The Belles of Etherington," *The Columbian Lady's and Gentleman's Magazine,* I (March, 1844), 125–30.

"The Blighted Heart," *Graham's Lady's and Gentleman's Magazine,* XXIII (July, 1843), 1–7.

"A Bride's Trials," *Columbian,* I (January, 1844), 22–25.

"Bush-Life," *The Union Magazine of Literature and Art,* VI (January, 1850), 70–74.

"A Chapter on Hospitality," *Godey's,* XXXII (May, 1846), 222–25.

"Concerts," *The Prairie Chicken,* No. 10 (July 1, 1865), 3.

"Conduct and Consequences: An Autobiography," *Graham's,* XXII (March, 1843), 150–57.

"Conversation," No. 1, *Union,* V (November, 1849), 292–96.

"Conversation," No. 2, *Union,* V (December, 1849), 369–71.

"The Country Funeral," *Union,* I (October, 1847), 179–81.

"Courting by Proxy: A Tale of New York," *Graham's,* XXIV (May, 1844), 215–18.

"The Dark Side," *Union,* VIII (January, 1851), 60–67.

"Detached Thoughts about England," *Union,* IV (February, 1849), 127–32.

"English and American Manners," *Union,* IV (June, 1849), 401–4.

"English Characteristics," *Union,* IV (May, 1849), 295–98.

"Essays on Works of Fiction: Written as a Preface to an Unpublished Novel," *The Prairie Chicken,* No. 11 (August 1, 1865), 4.

"Fastidiousness," *Union,* V (August, 1849), 102–6.

"Forest Literature," *Union,* II (May, 1848), 211–12.

"George Sand and the Journeyman Joiner," *Union,* I (November, 1847), 221–23.

"Goethe," *Union,* I (September, 1847), 127–29.

"Goethe's Education," *Union,* I (October, 1847), 168–69.

"Going into the Country Cures Baldness," *Godey's,* XXXIII (September, 1846), 109–12.

"The Great Prairie State," *The Continental Monthly Magazine,* III (May, 1863), 513–19.

"Growing Old Gracefully," *Union,* VIII (April, 1851), 257–62.

"The Hard Winter," *Union,* II (January, 1848), 43.

"Hints for an Essay on Presents," *Godey's,* XXX (January, 1845), 27–29.

"The Household," *Union,* VII (July, 1850), 42–46.

"Illinois in Spring-Time," *Atlantic Monthly,* II (September, 1858), 475–88.

"An Incident in Dream-Land," *Graham's,* XXII (June, 1843), 335–36.

"The Justice," *Union,* I (September, 1847), 114–16.

"Letter from Beaver Meadow, Pa.," *Knickerbocker's,* XVI (November, 1845), 409–13.

"The Lindleys; or Habits and Havings," *Godey's*, XXXIV (April, 1847), 193–98.

"Lion-Hunting," *Union*, VIII (February, 1851), 111–15.

"Literary Women," *Union*, VI (February, 1850), 150–54.

"The Log-House," *Union*, II (June, 1848), 274–75.

"The Log School-house," *Union*, VI (April, 1850), 251–56.

"London Streets—Livery Servants," *Union*, VIII (March, 1851), 159–64.

"A Love of a Singing Master," *Union*, II (March, 1848), 137–38.

"Mahomet," *Union*, VI (June, 1850), 411–16.

"Mistakes from Experience," *Arthur's Ladies' Magazine*, V (April, 1846), 187–90.

"Mrs. Pell's Pilgrimage," *Godey's*, XXXII (February, 1846), 61–66.

"The Mystery of Visiting," *Union*, VI (May, 1850), 317–21.

"New York" [No. 1], *Union*, IX (August, 1851), 147–51.

"New York" [No. 2], *Union*, IX (September, 1851), 203–6.

"Odds and Ends of Travel," *Union*, V (September, 1849), 139–42.

"Periodical Reading," *United States Magazine and Democratic Review*, XVI (January, 1845), 59–61.

"The Prince of Tezcuco: A Romance of Central America," *Columbian*, VII (January, 1847), 27–36.

"Prison Association—First Report of the Female Department of the Prison Association of New York," *Broadway Journal*, II (July 26, 1845), 45.

"Reading for Amusement," *Union*, VI (March, 1850), 192–96.

"Sight-seeing in Europe" [No. 1], *Union*, III (July, 1848), 1–5.

"Sight-seeing in Europe" [No. 2], *Union*, III (August, 1848), 49–54.

"Sight-seeing in Europe" [No. 3], *Union*, III (October, 1848), 145–51.

"Sight-seeing in Europe" [No. 4], *Union*, III (November, 1848), 193–99.

"Sight-seeing in Europe" [No. 5], *Union*, III (December, 1848), 241–46.

"Sight-seeing in Europe" [No. 6], *Union*, IV (January, 1849), 57–62.

"Sight-seeing in Europe" [No. 7], *Union*, IV (March, 1849), 181–85.

"Sight-seeing in Europe" [No. 8], *Union*, IV (April, 1849), 232–35.

"The Significance of Dress," No. 1, *Union*, VII (August, 1850), 99–102.

"The Significance of Dress," No. 2, *Union*, VII (September, 1850), 154–57.

"Sinecures; or, Parson Thacher's Day," *Columbian*, IV (July, 1845), 22–24.

"The Singing School," *Union*, I (December, 1847), 282–83.

"Sketch of a Case," *Graham's*, XXI (October, 1842), 187–91.

"Steps to Ruin," *Union,* I (November, 1847), 229–31.
"Streets of Paris—The Boulevards," *Union,* VIII (June, 1851), 401–5.
"Summer Recreation," No. 1, *Union,* VII (October, 1850), 243–47.
"Summer Recreation," No. 2, *Union,* VII (November, 1850), 261–66.
"Summer Recreation," No. 3, *Union,* VII (December, 1850), 370–72.
"Sunday in the Country," *Union,* II (April, 1848), 166–67.
"Thoughts on Education," No. 1, *Union,* V (July, 1849), 40–43.
"Thoughts on Education," No. 2, *Union,* V (October, 1849), 236–39.
"Town or Country?" *The Prairie Chicken,* No. 9 (June 1, 1865), 4.
"The Town Poor: A Western Reminiscence," *Arthur's,* V (January, 1846), 44–47.
"The Village School," *Union,* I (December, 1847), 45–48.
"Vincent Hervey, or the Man of Impulse," *Columbian,* II (August, 1844), 49–55.
"The Vision and the Creed of Piers Ploughman," *Columbian,* IV (November, 1845), 335–36.
"A Visit to Amelia Opie," *Peterson's Magazine,* XVII (March, 1850), 144–45.
"The Voiage and Travails of Sir John Maundeville," *Columbian,* V (February, 1846), 77–79.
"A Wedding in the Woods," *Godey's,* XXXVI (January, 1848), 2–5.
"What Must Be Must," *Columbian,* VI (September, 1846), 109–12.
"White Lies," *Peterson's,* XVII (April, 1850), 161–63.
"The World's Fair," *Union,* VIII (May, 1851), 321–26.

SECONDARY SOURCES

BOYNTON, PERCY H. *The Rediscovery of the Frontier.* Chicago: University of Chicago Press, 1931. The influence of the West on the writers of America—largely romantic during the first half of the nineteenth century. A reappraisal of the impact of the frontier on American writing, with emphasis on the major authors only.
DONDORE, DOROTHY A. *The Prairie and the Making of Middle America.* Cedar Rapids, Iowa: The Torch Press, 1926. An exemplary survey of the writers and their works in the cultural milieu of the Midwest. Several pages devoted to an estimate of Mrs. Kirkland's Western material, with comment on the realism of her sketches and her influence on later writers.
HALL, JAMES. *Legends of the West.* Philadelphia: Key and Biddle, 1833. One of the author's numerous collections of Western stories, written to appeal to readers unfamiliar with the scenes and the people; events are romantically portrayed.
HOFFMAN, CHARLES FENNO. *A Winter in the West.* 2 Vols. New York: Harper and Brothers, 1835. A journal of the author's wanderings

through the Midwest. Interesting in that his view of Michigan is so very different from Mrs. Kirkland's, both having traversed nearly identical routes.

KEYES, LANGLEY C. "Caroline M. Kirkland: A Pioneer in Realism." Unpublished Ph.D. dissertation, Harvard University, 1935. Careful, deliberate review of fiction and essays about the West which leads into a fine study of Mrs. Kirkland: her Western material, some of her magazine contributions as well. An emphasis on her realistic treatment of material, with many primary sources often quoted in their entirety. A valuable source for the student.

KIRKLAND, WILLIAM. "The West, the Paradise of the Poor," *United States Magazine and Democratic Review*, XV (August, 1844), 184–92. An indictment of the West by a man sobered by his experiences there, with humor often concealing the author's very real disenchantment: the contrast between the reality of Western life and the promise of life the West apparently offered.

KNUDSEN, LOUISE N. "Caroline Kirkland, Pioneer." Unpublished master's thesis, Michigan State College of Agriculture and Applied Science, 1934. Centered on Mrs. Kirkland's experiences in Michigan, with a number of primary sources often quoted in full. A sometimes arbitrary choice of Michigan material to substantiate the accuracy of Mrs. Kirkland's view of the West.

McCLOSKEY, JOHN C. "Back-Country Folkways in Mrs. Kirkland's *A New Home—Who'll Follow?*" *Michigan History*, XL (September, 1956), 297–308. One of a series of essays (title is explanatory) designed primarily to reacquaint the modern reader with Mrs. Kirkland. An emphasis on those aspects of *A New Home* where the author is best represented as a perceptive, sometimes caustic, commentator on the Michigan frontier she knew firsthand.

———. "Jacksonian Democracy in Mrs. Kirkland's *A New Home— Who'll Follow?*" *Michigan History*, XLV (December, 1961), 347– 52. One of a series of essays (title is explanatory) designed primarily to reacquaint the modern reader with Mrs. Kirkland. An emphasis on those aspects of *A New Home* where the author is best represented as a perceptive, sometimes caustic, commentator on the Michigan frontier she knew firsthand.

———. "Land Speculation in Michigan in 1835–36 as Described in Mrs. Kirkland's *A New Home—Who'll Follow?*," *Michigan History*, XLII (March, 1958), 26–34. One of a series of essays (title is explanatory) designed primarily to reacquaint the modern reader with Mrs. Kirkland. An emphasis on those aspects of *A New Home* where the author is best represented as a perceptive, sometimes caustic, commentator on the Michigan frontier she knew firsthand.

McDERMOTT, JOHN FRANCIS, ed. Washington Irving, *A Tour on the Prairies*. Norman: University of Oklahoma Press, 1962. A romantic apostrophe to the American West, an account of the author's trip through the Midwest in the company of Indian commissioners. Edited for the modern reader with critical comment.

NERBER, JOHN, ed. Caroline M. Kirkland, *A New Home or Life in the Clearings*. New York: G. P. Putnam, 1953. A compilation of the best of Mrs. Kirkland's Western material, with *A New Home* reproduced in full. Edited for the modern reader with an introduction.

OSBORNE, WILLIAM S., ed. Caroline M. Kirkland, *A New Home—Who'll Follow?* New Haven: College and University Press, 1965. An edition which follows Mrs. Kirkland's second (1840) edition of the book; the material in the introduction is substantially the same as that which appears in Chapter 2 of this study.

PATTEE, FRED LEWIS. *The Feminine Fifties*. New York: D. Appleton-Century Company, 1940. An appreciative study of the popular women writers when their influence was most largely felt in mid-century American fiction. Not so much a discussion of individual writers as it is a comment on literary trends and tastes of the times.

RUSK, RALPH L. *The Literature of the Middle Western Frontier*. 2 Vols. New York: Columbia University Press, 1926. Definitive literary history of the writers and their works with perceptive and scholarly comment. An ageless reference for the student, but only appreciative and superficial statements about Mrs. Kirkland.

TWAMLEY, EDNA M. "The Western Sketches of Caroline Mathilda (Stansbury) Kirkland," *Michigan Historical Collections*, XXXIX (1915), 89–124. The pioneer essay (a master's thesis which has been slightly edited) in which the author proves the truthfulness of Mrs. Kirkland's observations about life in the Michigan wilderness.

Index

Names of characters and places in Mrs. Kirkland's writings are followed by the title—in parenthesis—of the work in which they appear.